Recovery
in the Torah

MOSAICA PRESS

Recovery in the Torah

Models of Spirituality and Healing

Rabbi Chaim Meyer Tureff, EdD

Published by Mosaica Press, Inc.
www.mosaicapress.com
info@mosaicapress.com

SOBERMAN'S™
—Estate—

In honor of

Jeff Prager and Dr. Jerry Josen

May their memory be a blessing.

Soberman's Estate was founded in honor of two adult Jewish men, Jeff Prager and Dr. Jerry Josen, who passed away from addiction and alcoholism. Jeff Prager was the brother of and Dr. Jerry Josen was the best friend of the founder of Soberman's Estate, Mitch Prager.
Soberman's Estate is a state-licensed, nationally accredited, world-class residential treatment and wellness center for adult men to recover from alcoholism, addiction, and behavioral health issues.

https://www.sobermansestate.com/
Info@SobermansEstate.com
480.595.2222

Dedicated in loving memory
to our son

Evan

Who was blessed with a beautiful soul and a sweet gentle nature
that will always be remembered and forever missed

Congratulations, Rabbi T.
Your book connects the spiritual
with the psychological, the heart with the mind,
to the wonders and wisdom of Torah in a unique
and relatable way.

ANGEL AND ALAN, *z"l*, SCHNEIDER

In the merit of our beloved son,
brother, nephew, cousin, uncle, and friend

Adam Aroose (Adam *ben* Daneal), *a"h*

Who lived from his warm heart, may the words of this book
enter readers' hearts and inspire healing. We often have the
misconception that the dark places in life, addiction being one
of the darkest, is a place where Hashem does not go, a place
from which one must crawl out of the trenches alone. I pray that
through this book, people see that Hashem lets us know that
there is a place for healing through Torah. Contrary to popular
belief, one is absolutely NOT expected to heal completely
outside the context of Torah and only come to God once he is
"good enough." The truth is, Hashem is in the darkness with us
regardless, and it's up to us if we want to acknowledge his
company and use that relationship to strengthen, heal, and
come back to our true selves. May this book be a tool for those
suffering, healing, witnessing, helping, or even simply learning
to bring Hashem into the process of addiction recovery.

YESHIVA CHONEN DAAS
Ramat Bet Shemesh

ו' אדר ב', תשפ"ב
March 9, 2022

בס"ד

Dear Rabbi Tureff,

Thank you for the opportunity to review your *sefer* **Recovery in the Torah.** Your examples of Biblical Addiction successfully proves that such an analysis is not to be feared. Each analysis of the anomalies of rational behavior is well thought out. The proofs you bring to those who rely on the principle of faith to overcome addiction are not based on dogma.

Although Biblical Addiction described in the Torah has its roots dating back to a time before internet and rampant substance abuse made available by drug cartels, the case studies are relevant today. Rabbi Tureff has taken this very broad subject and successfully blended Chazal and well known secular programs, for example the well known 12 Step Program used by Alcoholics Anonymous, in a way which builds a solid foundation of faith that the entire Torah was given from Hashem to Moses on Mount Sinai. Readers will find the crossover engaging whether or not one has a background in Torah learning.

This *sefer* is a must for someone who works in the field of kiruv and healing those afflicted with addiction. Rabbi Tureff bases his insights on well known Torah Scholars and delivers them in a way which will immediately capture the attention of a person seeking the truth and healing.

This *sefer* is well sourced and a reflection of your commitment to Torah and your overwhelming desire to heal others. May you merit seeing your *sefer*, **Recovery in the Torah,** warmly received and well circulated amongst *Klal Yisrael.*

With Torah blessings and warmest regards,

Rabbi Daniel Channen

Rabbi Daniel Channen
Rosh Yeshiva
Yeshiva Chonen Daas

Nachal Refaim 34a Ramat Bet Shemesh, 99096, Israel
USA: 914-826-8686 Israel: 054-801-5821
Website: ChonenDaas.org Email: RabbiChannen@gmail.com

Rabbi Shaya Karlinsky

Rabbi Tureff's book is directed to those in recovery from addictions. There are many important messages that Rabbi Tureff presents, creating connections with the weekly Torah portions. On the surface, these lessons are directed to recovering addicts. So the average person may not think there is much of value for him or her. "I may have challenges, but substance addiction isn't one of them."

But Rabbi Dr. Abraham Twerski, z"l, in his book *Addictive Thinking,* has shown us that the underlying causes of addiction have taken root in our society. Our culture is one that facilitates the same kind of thinking that leads to substance addiction. The drive for immediate gratification, distorted thinking, low self-esteem, victimhood, denial, and rationalizations are all prevalent in our modern culture and affect our daily lives. These problems may not lead to substance abuse, but they clearly undermine our ability for spiritual growth.

Read with that in mind, Rabbi Tureff's messages to recovering addicts and those involved with those facilitating that recovery can serve as a guide and motivator for anyone looking to grow as a more spiritual and productive person.

Rabbi Shaya Karlinsky
Jerusalem

Rabbi Hanoch Teller

In this searingly powerful collection of thoughts on the weekly Torah portion, Rabbi Dr. Chaim Tureff shares with us a new perspective. Just as an educator or a parent will be rewarded by reading special education literature, a conscientious individual will richly profit from Rabbi Tureff's insights from the perspective of a recovering addict.

Frankly, *Recovery in the Torah* is a haunting, and—pun not intended—sobering revelation of how Torah messages can assist with recovery. Even one who has never been tempted by prohibited substances can reap deep benefits from *Recovery in the Torah*. The Torah direly forbids bizarre and appalling—seemingly never tempting—pagan rites, for it realizes that there is a dark place that may lurk inside the heart and in the psyche.

The malaise of addiction permeates society ubiquitously but also insidiously. Few are knowledgeable, or astute enough, to detect the tell-tale symptoms, which puts us all at risk to being victimized by a mindset that is anything but Torahitic. Hence, we are indebted to Rabbi Chaim Tureff for not only his enlightening and memorable commentary, but also for sharpening our focus to be aware of thoughts and behavior that may mirror the destructive path of an addict.

We all sorely miss the illumination and instruction of Rabbi Doctor Abraham J. Twerski; I venture that he would applaud the appearance of this volume.

Rabbi Hanoch Teller

Table of Contents

Parshiyos

Holidays

Acknowledgments

I acknowledge with gratitude the support and guidance of those who helped me complete this vital project.

First, I want to thank Hashem for giving me the guidance, ability, and desire to carry out such important work. Addiction is something that has had an impact on my life since I came into this world. I have seen and experienced the devastation it can have upon those it affects. But, I have also seen the stories of redemption and renewal. The holy Torah is the source for everything, and the seventy facets allow those to see special glimmers of light that impact each individual in their time and place. We meet the Torah where we are. Thank You, Hashem, for allowing me this opportunity to learn, grow, and hopefully be able to give back to others.

I want to thank all the people who contributed to making sure this publication happened, including individual donors who felt this was an important endeavor and to Mosaica Press for publishing a book about this important but often neglected topic within the Jewish community. I want to give special thanks to Rabbi Asher Brander for guiding me towards Mosaica Press and Rabbi Adam Kligfeld for his guidance and important logistical support.

I want to thank Angel and Alan, *z"l*, Schneider and Cheyenne and Ivy Rose for your support. G-d willing, Evan's beautiful soul, *z"l*, will continue to be illuminated through this work. May we continue to learn and grow from those who have passed away from this disease.

I want to thank Malkie, Amanda, and Jessica Aroose, in addition to the Grunfeld, Bohorodzaner, and Love families, for your support. May Adam's special soul find peace, love, and support through this work. May Adam's warmth and smile continue to illuminate those who miss his presence.

I want to give thanks to my sister and brother for their support. My sister has been in the trenches with me since the beginning. Your love, support, and friendship have been invaluable. And I would also like to thank my sons, Eliyahu Nadiv and Tzion Adir, who both bring so much joy to my life. My time with you is often interrupted and sometimes shared with people you have never met. You understand that I have meetings, need to lead groups, and must make time to write and listen to other people. Eliyahu, the warmth and generosity of your soul is special and will serve you well. Tzion, your deep introspection and humor are guiding principles that make those who know you feel special.

My sincerest thanks and deepest heartfelt appreciation go to my *zivug,* my wife, Karyn Grunfeld. Thank you for always supporting me in this endeavor and all the work that I do in addiction recovery, even when it means having strangers in our home, that I have to meet with someone at odd hours, or that I have to work on my days off which means extra work for you. I appreciate your love, encouragement, flexibility, and emotional support.

Introduction

There is an addiction epidemic that has struck the world at large and specifically the United States. According to conservative estimates, over twenty percent of Americans are addicted to drugs, alcohol, sex, gambling, or food. This does not include addictions to the Internet, shopping, work, anger, or nicotine, which would make the numbers astronomical (Sederer, 2015). These numbers are infiltrating into the Jewish community (Sucaray, 2013). According to *Psychology Today*,

> *addiction is a condition that results when a person ingests a substance (e.g., alcohol, cocaine, nicotine) or engages in an activity (e.g., gambling, sex, shopping) that can be pleasurable but the continued use/act of which becomes compulsive and interferes with ordinary life responsibilities, such as work, relationships, or health. Users may not be aware that their behavior is out of control and causing problems for themselves and others.*

In 1935 in Akron, Ohio, the first ever meeting of Alcoholics Anonymous (AA) took place with Bill Wilson and his friend, and the 12 Steps of Recovery became a reality. This was the first time that addiction was seen through a lens of spirituality and mind and not just an action which was done by a "bad person" or caused by a negative personality trait. Through the new definition of addiction, it was not seen as just an "allergy" but instead as a mind, body, and soul issue. These findings have been documented through scientific studies and data (Steinberg 2015). AA is full of general spiritual connotations without being associated with a specific religion, as one can see in Steps 2 and 3: "Came to believe that a power greater than ourselves could restore us to sanity" and "Made a decision to turn our will and our lives over to the care of God as we understood Him" (Bill W., 1981, p. 5).

There is no magic pill or one way to cure an addict. There are many different ways that people try to become sober from their addictions. The 12 Steps is just one highly successful way, but it might not work for everyone (Steinberg, 2015). According to conservative estimates, fifty to ninety percent of all addicts will relapse. The National Institute of Drug Abuse estimates that between forty to eighty percent of drug addicts will relapse according to their 2015 findings.

There have been a number of rehab centers and organizations that have opened up the last forty years which are Jewish faith-based rehab centers. These centers are located in New York, Florida, California, and Israel, among other places. For many observant Jews, they need to make sure the 12 Steps are consistent with their values, which is not always the case with secular ideology or values which are not directly based in the Torah. Rabbi Dr. Abraham Twerski, z"l, gave the original *heter,* or rabbinical permission, for the 12 Steps (Twerski, 2010). There was some concern about applying modern psychology to a spiritual practice.

Rabbi Dr. Abraham Twerski was one of the most important people in dealing with addiction in Orthodox Jewish literature and secular literature. He opened Gateway Rehabilitation Center in 1972, a treatment center for alcohol and chemical dependency. Not only did he serve as the Clinical Therapist, but he was also a Rabbi. He wrote a number of books dealing with addiction. He also did a great deal of work integrating the 12 Steps and Judaism (Twerski, 2016). Most importantly Rabbi Twerski told the observant Orthodox Jewish community that the 12-Step program was a valuable tool in treating addiction. This gave the community permission to follow the 12 Steps without feeling that they were compromising their religious practices.

Rabbi Dr. Twerski was a pioneer in the field of recovery. His books integrate spirituality and Torah-related approaches in a subtle and benign way. By focusing on spirituality and concepts that are relatable to the Torah, he integrates Jewish spirituality, Jewish ritual, and the 12 Steps. Self-reflection and introspection are key in the 12 Steps, spirituality, and Judaism (Heinze, 1999). Rabbi Twerski was guided towards the 12-Step program by a patient he had. Once he investigated and learned more about AA, he was very touched by two key components of the program. The first was the equality related to everyone in the program (Twerski, 2000). Everyone was equal in the room, unlike religion where sometimes donors, status, family history, and other things play a role in how someone is perceived. There is no hierarchy in the 12 Steps. The second thing that moved Rabbi Twerski was the dedication that people in the program had for one another (Twerski, 2000). There is a true sense of giving and selflessness. The program teaches that to truly be in recovery one must give of oneself (Bill W., 1981).

Parshiyos

Bereishis

In this seminal Torah reading, we learn about the creation of the world and, in particular, of human beings. There are so many intense questions, and there is so much complexity to this parashah (Torah reading).

When Hashem is describing the creation of a partner for Adam HaRishon, the first person created in the Torah, the Torah verse states, "It is not good that man should be alone; I will make him a helper opposite him." The question is asked by the ancient Sages: What is meant by a "helper opposite him"? *Rashi*, a medieval French commentator and rabbi, states that it means if Adam HaRishon, and in turn, all men are worthy, their partner is just that—a partner, and if not, then they are opposite him—a constant source of enmity.

According to *Bereishis Rabbah*, the Midrash (ancient commentary) on *Bereishis*, "One who has no wife…is not a whole man." This seems to put an abundant amount of pressure and importance on having a partner. Life's a journey that is very challenging, with many peaks and valleys. It is difficult enough for man to navigate these challenges, but with a partner whom one can trust, he has someone with whom he can work.

This is the same in the world of recovery and rehab. One is not asked to try to become sober on his own. It is a difficult task to go through recovery by yourself. That is why it is important—and some say imperative—to have a sponsor as you are starting on the road of recovery. It allows you to have someone who is an "*ezer kenegdo*," a helper opposite you. This is a partner, someone who can guide you through the trials and tribulations of sobriety. Throughout recovery, there are peaks and valleys as well. There are questions, and there are struggles. The sponsor can help clarify what is going on, since he has been there himself. He might not have been down the exact same road that you are on, but he understands the struggles that you are enduring. A sponsor's job is not to acquiesce to your every need, but to challenge you and look out for your best interests.

This is similar to a spouse. There is not always agreement, with slow romantic walks on the beach. Instead, your partner will question you when you might be making foolish decisions, and he or she might not always agree with you. It is a partnership. So too, with a sponsor, his job is to push you to new levels and to help you become a new version of yourself. If you are the same person who you were when you got married, then one can question the success and depth of the relationship. It is no different with a sponsor. The job is to challenge the status quo and encourage continuous growth on a daily basis. As the previous Lubavitcher Rebbe stated, "I'm not satisfied for my work to just 'continue'—it must increase! Every living thing must grow!"

Noach

Imagine a world where you are all alone. As you look to your right and left, there is no one remaining. From the ashes of destruction, you are asked to make something from nothing. As those who lost their entire family and everything that they owned in the Holocaust know all too well, it is a difficult task to just move on from such a scenario.

Noach was faced with similar circumstances. His extended family, every acquaintance, and member of society was dead. In fact, everyone and everything around him had died, and he was tasked with keeping humanity going after the great flood. He was not only asked to spend decades making a boat, but suffered ridicule for building the boat. Most of these difficulties intensified as Noach was on the ark for over a year. He was stuck on the Ark with his wife, children, and their spouses. And, of course, a bunch of animals.

Once he was able to exit the Ark, one of the first things that Noach chose to do was to plant a vineyard. This vineyard enabled him to make wine and, eventually, get drunk. The text proceeds to tell us that Noach not only got drunk, but something happened with his son Cham, which had dire consequences for everyone involved. According to one Rabbinic source, Noach was sodomized while he was drunk, while another source states that he was castrated by his son. This traumatic event changed the trajectory of Noach's life and that of his children.

As any addict knows, in the face of extreme adversity, it seems very natural to go to one's substance of choice to help numb the pain. It is part of normative culture that people smoke, drink alcohol, consume some edibles, or go shopping to help alleviate stressful experiences or to just "take the edge off.' But, as anybody who has struggled with addiction has experienced, "One is too many and a thousand is never enough." The best way to work through difficult situations is to face them head on, not to run away from them by dulling oneself to the pain. By not facing the situation at hand, people add another layer of complexity to their already difficult situation.

No one can blame Noach for struggling with his situation. The question is: Could he have made a better choice to work out his problems? The 12 Steps of any recovery program offer a number of things that an addict can try in order to work through difficulties that come up in life. Through prayer, being of service to other people, journaling, and working on the first step of the 12 Steps (e.g., "We are powerless over…and our life is unmanageable"), we have some tools to move forward from the depths of despair. These are tools that anyone, whether in recovery or not, can use when battling pain and despair. When one decides, instead, to drown his sorrows in an array of addictive actions, there is never a good outcome. And as Noach experienced, these addictions can cause damage beyond the person using, with repercussions that can impact family structures, communities, and even generations to come.

Lech Lecha

Did you ever move when you were young? There was a new place to live, a new school, new friends, and, of course, uncertainty. As a matter of fact, moving is seen as one of the three most stressful things that a person can endure. It's so scary to go on a journey and not know where you are going. You don't have directions or a road map. How are you going to get there and what will happen when you arrive?

When Hashem spoke to Avraham and told him to move from the place of his birth, he faced this exact struggle. All Avraham ever knew was Ur Kasdim, and his family, friends, and life that was there. The Rabbis note that Avraham was given ten tests by Hashem, and being told to leave his home and everything familiar was one of those tests. In *Pirkei Avos* 5:4, we find that Avraham's ability to pass these tests was seen as a litmus test for his being chosen to lead monotheism, according to the Maharal of Prague. Some commentators count Avraham having to leave everything behind as the first test. By leaving his past and moving forward, Avraham showed faith in Hashem and the ability to follow direction.

As anyone in recovery knows, when one starts the journey, there is a *Lech Lecha*-type moment. The past and everything that you have done is placed behind you, and you must journey somewhere that you have never been. It is a place of uncertainty. While in active addiction, everything you do is colored and impacted by the addiction, be it dating, working, and even sleeping. You are now embarking on a new journey without your trusted companion. And much like Avraham, this is a test from Hashem. Are you willing to leave everything behind you and move forward to a place where Hashem will guide you, where you will need to have faith and trust? You will need to go somewhere that you have never been. This test is not an easy one, but one that, much like Avraham, will change the entire trajectory of your life. The road to recovery and sobriety calls for you to make changes, to see the world differently, and to know that you are not alone. It's important for you to realize that going from your place to a new one is something that many people have done before you and succeeded. So put your foot forward, trust the process, and know that, just as Hashem was with Avraham in this test, He is with you in yours. Just make sure that you are wearing comfortable shoes because the journey is long but rewarding.

Vayeira

I remember when I was young, and I thought that I could do something. Everyone else around me did not believe that I could do it. All my friends doubted me, and I may even have questioned my own ability to succeed at the task. Eventually, I gave up because I did not see success as a possibility.

In *Parashas Vayeira*, Avraham and Sarah are visited by angels who come to tell them that, at a hundred and at ninety years old respectively, they were about to have a child. Avraham laughed with joy while Sarah initially laughed with disbelief, "After I have withered, will I have smooth skin? And my husband is old!" According to *Rashi*, Sarah did not believe that she could still physically have a child, having seen how her body had changed and aged. So she was dismissive of the news. She also had endured years of barrenness, during which her maidservant, Hagar, had a child from Avraham. So, it made sense that Sarah had given up hope and did not believe the news.

This is similar to someone in recovery from addiction. Many times, all the signs that the person has seen and experienced in his life lead him to feel hopeless. He feels like he has gone down another dead-end road with nowhere to turn. The person does not feel that there is any way he can find sobriety. Every avenue seems closed and every time he tries to get sober, he experiences failure. Just as Sarah no longer had physical signs that would make it possible for her to have a child, the addict, too, sees physical signs in his life that convince him that he is beyond help; things such as a loss of relationships, a job, a house, money, or his health. Many times, when an addict finally meets someone who is in recovery, he listens with a sense of loss and impossibility at the notion of becoming sober. But, as Step 2 of Alcoholics Anonymous notes, "We came to believe a power greater than ourselves can restore us to sanity." That's right, something greater than ourselves is able to perform open miracles and lead us on a path of sobriety. If the person would trust that Hashem is there for him and believe that sobriety is possible, open miracles would occur. Just as Sarah was able to have a child when she was old, after years of barrenness, so too, Hashem gives those struggling with addiction the opportunity to find a new life and new hope as they walk the path of recovery.

Chayei Sarah

Being a part of a funeral is never a pleasant experience. There are many raw emotions that can come out; old family pain and issues that tend to boil to the surface. Unresolved issues, whether within the family generally or with the deceased specifically, can cause even more pain than the actual death. The pain is palpable for everyone involved. Sometimes this causes people to not be their best selves at these difficult moments.

But what about those who take the opportunity to do some reflection and use death as a chance to substantially change? In the parashah, Avraham dies and the verse states, "And his sons Yitzchak and Yishmael buried him in the Cave of Machpelah..." What the rabbis notice about the verse is how Yitzchak, the younger son of Avraham, is first and then Yishmael is named. The rabbis say that this indicates that Yishmael repented from his earlier transgressions and gave proper honor to Yitzchak.

This sort of repentance is commendable, but not shocking for those who are in recovery from substances, food, or any addictive activity. As part of recovery, one is constantly self-reflecting. It is part of the process. The eighth and ninth steps of the 12-Step program deal with making amends with those whom we have hurt, and it is not just lip service. One cannot expect to gain full sobriety without letting go of the past and changing one's ways. Saying sorry and making restitution where possible is part of the process. Part of repenting is not only saying sorry, but also changing one's actions, especially in a situation where one has the opportunity to make the same mistake again.

Through his actions at Avraham's funeral, Yishmael proved that he was a changed man. Walk into any 12-Step meeting and you will literally see hundreds of women and men who have also made this discovery: to truly change, one has to look into his heart, make a pledge to change, and then back up that pledge with action. Someone who is sober is constantly placed in situations where he might lose his sobriety, but by working on his recovery, even in the most difficult moments, like Yishmael, he will be able to stay sober and pass these tests with flying colors.

Toldos

Have you ever ordered a sweet and sour dish only to find out that it was either too sweet or too sour? There was not that perfect balance but instead an extreme. In this week's parashah, Rivkah finally became pregnant with twins after waiting ten years to get pregnant. She struggled as her pregnancy was not going particularly well. She was in tremendous pain and the Torah notes that there appeared to be a struggle with her twins. The commentaries explain that whenever Rivkah walked past a place full of spirituality, Yaakov would stir, while when she walked past a place of idolatry or ill repute, Esav would stir. They note that the twins were struggling within the womb for dominance.

When they were older, both brothers would receive a blessing from their father Yitzchak. They were told that when one son was in charge, the other son would be on the bottom; they wouldn't be ruling at the same time together. This is a perfect metaphor for addiction.

As recovering addicts know, there is no balance when it comes to being in active addiction and recovery. When one is actively using, it becomes the ruling force in his life. Whether it is at work, with family and friends, or during everyday activities, the addiction dictates one's course of action. Whereas those in active recovery know that when one is sober from whatever force that he was struggling against, recovery becomes the ruling force in one's life, ruling everything that he does, regardless of whether it directly involves recovery.

Esav and Yaakov were similar to active addiction and recovery in the sense of good and evil. When one was ruling, it was impossible for the other to have any power. The nature of each one's presence was such that it dominated to such a degree that the other brother was nullified by the sheer presence of his brother. Even though they both would exist simultaneously, they did not work hand in hand but truly opposed one another. The rabbis go so far as to state that when the Jewish people are doing what they are supposed to be doing, Esav is unable to rule. Again, with an addiction recovery program, when someone is working through the steps of the program, following directions, going to meetings, and being of service, recovery rules. Just as Esav and Yaakov did not work hand and hand and only one of them could lead at the same time, so it is with recovery. If you are sober, your addiction is not ruling, but more importantly, when your addiction is ruling, your sobriety is nowhere to be found. It unfortunately is being ruled by your addiction.

Vayetzei

I'll never forget the Saturday morning sleepover when I found out Andy was moving to Texas. A cool guy whom I loved hanging out with; we played baseball together and were the best of friends. We had a blast playing video games together and hanging out. It was as if a part of me left when he moved. He was a good friend, and his presence was missed once he left.

The parashah starts by noting that Yaakov left Be'er Sheva and went to Charan. What is the purpose in telling us that he left? According to *Rashi*, when a righteous person, a *tzaddik*, leaves a place it makes an impression on that place. As *Rashi* states, the *tzaddik* brings guidance, spirituality, and importance to the place. The *tzaddik* helps bring stability, balance, and holiness. Once they leave, there is a void left behind.

This is similar to the role that a sponsor plays in recovery. A sponsor is a mentor or a guide who has been in recovery and worked through the steps and no longer has to use. He is a role model for recovery. That's it—nothing more, nothing less. Yet, the sponsor plays a prominent role in the recovery of the addict. He can help with the big and small details, ranging from what is the best meeting to attend, to budgeting and paying bills on time, to being a listening ear at 3:00 am. The sponsor is able to help the addict navigate every step of the way. The support is truly endless.

Firstly, a sponsor has been there before. He has walked the path to sobriety. Secondly, he has done something right which has helped guide his sobriety. He didn't become sober through magic, he worked the steps and did what was necessary to get on the right path. Third and most importantly, he is a role model. When done correctly, much like a *tzaddik* who brings stability and G-dliness to a location, the sponsor can bring the same to the addict. A sponsor literally can save your life. He brings the sustenance to move the addict forward physically, spiritually, mentally, and emotionally. This is a role that is just as important as the one that a *tzaddik* plays.

Vayishlach

I remember the wrestling matches in the yard with my older sibling. He would always use his superior strength and knowledge to get the upper hand. No matter what I did, he would always seem to win. Until that one day, when I finally was able to get him off, and I prevailed. Once that happened, our relationship shifted. He saw me as an equal or, at least, not as "lowly." This helped make me feel better about myself and was a source of pride.

In *Vayishlach*, Yaakov encounters an angel. The story states that he was going back to get some things that his family had left behind. During this journey, he encountered an angel, and they wrestled the entire evening. It was a fierce back-and-forth battle. Although neither seemed to prevail, the angel made a physical impediment on Yaakov that stayed with him for life. The angel requested that Yaakov let go of him so he could lead prayers with Hashem. The wrestling match changed things for Yaakov, including getting the name Yisrael (Israel). This was a shift in how Yaakov saw himself. As Yaakov states, "Because I saw Hashem face to face, and my soul was saved."

This entire episode is similar to the struggle that an addict goes through. Almost every recovering addict had his own wrestling match that he had to surmount before he was on the road to sobriety. This "aha moment" might have been when he hit bottom, and he was finally able to wrestle his struggles and turn the corner towards sobriety. This "aha" moment is one about which the addict can later tell you very specific details, including things like the day, time, who, what, when, and where. This moment was when he wrestled with his addiction, and he finally overcame the initial struggle. It doesn't mean that he didn't continue to struggle or that he was sober, but it was that moment where his ability to wrestle with his addiction allowed him to know that there is a road to recovery. This moment, just like Yaakov's with the angel, is a spiritual moment even if the addict did not see it as such at the time. It can retroactively be seen by the addict as that moment, along a journey of many moments, which aided in his recovery. Like Yaakov's struggle, the entire episode might even include emotional and physical scars, but that struggle was a necessary part of the road to change and recovery.

Vayeishev

There is a saying that everything happens for a reason. There are numerous stories about things happening that seem frustrating, annoying, or downright painful that, ultimately, turn out for the best. At the moment, we don't always have the insight to understand or even accept that what is happening is for the best, but if we are able to keep faith, many times we end up seeing the wisdom and divine guidance in the trials and tribulations that we experience.

In *Parashas Vayeishev*, Yosef is sold by his brothers. This was after they threw him into a pit and contemplated killing him. This was some very intense sibling rivalry. Through later parshiyos, we understand that the pain that Yosef went through was ultimately not only a benefit for him, but for the entire Jewish people. Later, during a severe famine, Yosef's entire family moved down to Egypt and was saved because Yosef became a leader in Egypt. Eventually, this all became clear, but not for twenty-two years. That is a long time for anyone to wait in order to clearly see the difficulty that he encountered in his life. Although it took time, Yosef would come to understand that the tests that he encountered were for the best.

A person who is in active addiction thinks about the pain and suffering that he is experiencing. Many times, he questions why he was plagued by such an affliction. How could Hashem put him in a situation that is so painful? He wishes that he never had to encounter such trials and tribulations because, quite honestly, sometimes they are severe. Yet, once one is able to attain sobriety, he sees life through an entirely new lens. He understands that it is possible that his struggles with addiction were placed upon him so that he can be able to help other people.

Anyone can help a recovering addict, but someone who has encountered the struggles of addiction can help on another level. Such a person has unique insights. Much like Yosef, he is a leader in the field. He has distinct gifts and abilities to help someone struggling with addiction in a way that others are unable to do. If Yosef did not live in Egypt and was not a leader, would B'nei Yisrael have been saved? We cannot know, but their chances increased dramatically once Yosef had the power to help them. Ultimately, Yosef told his brothers that it was all part of Hashem's plan and that he held no ill will towards them for their actions. Those who manage to become sober have similar feelings. They do not wish for other people to go through the same challenges that they went through, but they are grateful for what they went through because it was only through that experience that they are now able to help other people and to see life in a different way.

Mikeitz

As all adults know, things don't necessarily happen as quickly as we want. Children kick and scream (as do some adults) when they don't get what they want right away. Sometimes, we might wait for what seems like an eternity before getting what we would like. And then there are those things we want which we might not ever get. In our instant gratification society, waiting for anything can be tedious. We look for something online, we expect that we can order it and get it delivered immediately. We get frustrated when our internet goes down, when we don't get our food quick enough, and when people make us wait for a response when we message them.

Yosef felt this impatience as he sat in jail for years for a crime that he did not commit. Yet, in an instant, Pharaoh called for him, and so began his new life of freedom. According to Sforno—Ovadia ben Yaakov Sforno, a fifteenth-century Italian commentator—the alacrity of Yosef's freedom was due to Hashem's desire and ability to cause salvation to happen instantaneously.

This instantaneous resolution to a problem is one for which we all hope. Recovering addicts sometimes struggle for years to get sober. They take two steps forward and then three steps back. This yo-yo ride is a struggle in perseverance. Just as Yosef desired to leave jail, so too, does an addict desire to leave the jail of addiction that engulfs his life. This movement from "jail" to future "freedom" can happen instantaneously. Why does it occur so quickly? Many times, an addict will seek recovery after he has hit the proverbial rock bottom. This is a situation so bad, so dangerous, and so filled with despair that the only place for him to go is up. This could start him on the road to recovery, but sobriety might not be obtained for some time. What makes it become the last time? Why is this time different from any other? Why is it that, at that point, an addict finally becomes sick and tired of being sick and tired? As many addicts know, this salvation might never come. But there is an opportunity, where that key finally unlocks the door to recovery. This instantaneous salvation, like Yosef's, didn't happen overnight, but the freedom did. After years of struggle and pain, the addict finally turns the corner and sees the light ahead. He enjoys the freedom of a life without the shackles of his addiction.

Vayigash

Most children love dressing up in costumes. Some adults enjoy it as well. You get to pretend to be whoever you want to be. Your favorite superhero, animal, or Biblical character. There are all kinds of props you can use, including the ability to act like your character. Children are notorious for dressing up, especially when it's their bedtime or at other inopportune times.

Sometimes, we don't necessarily wear a costume for fun, but out of necessity. Yosef was playing that role in *Parashas Vayigash*. As he was second in command in Egypt, leading Pharaoh's kingdom, Yosef never made contact with his family. It had been over twenty years since he had seen them. When his brothers came to Egypt, he went through an entire ruse before finally revealing his true identity. At the right moment, he said to them, "I am your brother Yosef, whom you sold to Egypt...," and, of course, there was embarrassment and trepidation from his brothers when they realized who he was. Ultimately though, there was relief, and the entire family, including Yosef's father, moved to Egypt. This seminal moment in the history of the Jewish people set off a chain of events that lead to slavery, redemption, and revelation—remarkable consequences for the family and all of Israel, which were due to the unmasking of Yosef.

The addict has a similar unmasking that changes the course of his life. For those who have hidden their addiction, the seminal moment, when they reveal what was going on behind the mask, can be full of emotions, including fear, trepidation, and ultimately, relief. The ruse is over, and they are able to take the necessary steps to move forward in their life. The unmasking of their true identity will not be without bumps and bruises along the way. Just as Israel descends into slavery before ultimately being redeemed, so too, the addict will travel a difficult journey on his road to recovery. There are people who were hurt, relationships that need to be repaired, self-reflection that can be painful, and sometimes, financial consequences that need attending. It goes without saying that the path for a recovering addict, much like B'nei Yisrael in Egypt, might be filled with challenges, but ultimately, coming clean, doing the work, and forging a new path will lead to personal redemption. This new reality might not be one that the addict ever could have imagined, but it is one filled with promise, hope, and sobriety.

Vayechi

Selflessness is not such an easy attribute to master. Many psychologists note that everyone does things for ulterior motives. How will this benefit me? How will this make me look? How does this make me feel?

In *Parashas Vayechi*, right before his death, Yaakov asks to see his son Yosef. He knows he is about to pass away, and he asks his son to please bury him with his ancestors in Israel. Yaakov explicitly states that this favor is called "kindness and truth." The ancient rabbis explained that "kindness and truth" refer to kindness for people who are dead; this is a genuine kindness because one cannot be repaid and doesn't do such a kindness in order to be repaid. The Talmud in *Mo'ed Katan* (28A) says, "He who eulogizes will be eulogized; he who buries will be buried." Rabbi Zvi Yehudah notes that no one looks forward to this type of payment.

There are few things in life that one does without wanting some sort of reciprocation. Being of service and a sponsor in the 12-Step program is a case of someone giving without wanting anything in return. When one answers a call at two in the morning for someone in a program, or shows up to support someone in a program, or allows someone from a program to stay with him because the person has nowhere else to go, the person doing that kindness doesn't seek any sort of reciprocity. We know from the steps in a recovery program that part of getting sober is to be of service. It is similar to eating, sleeping, and breathing. You don't want to wake up at five in the morning in a hotel surrounded by drug paraphernalia and realize that you never went home and only then reach out to someone in the program. The person who answers the call, or shows up to help you get dressed, wants what's best for you. The thought of repayment doesn't even enter his head. Instead, he is one hundred percent there for you, to be of service to you, to help you, and to get you on the path to sobriety. There are no payments, no promissory notes, and no amount of "kindness and truth" that the person does that can be repaid. He is saving a life and in turn, helping create new lives. The person never thinks about wanting to be in the same situation where he can call upon you for this same support. Just as we don't want to think about the day of our death, we don't want to think about when we might be struggling or even using and needing support. A person does it so that he can be of service. The next time you are doing something for someone in a program or you are being helped by someone in a program, remember this is "kindness and truth"!

Shemos

Confidence is a funny thing. Some people seem to be born with it, while others struggle their entire life trying to access some form of confidence. Whether it is a job they don't think they can do, a potential partner who seems out of their league, or an area of knowledge that they feel that they don't have the ability to understand, they struggle with confidence, even when given an opportunity to do something special.

In *Shemos*, Moshe had this exact issue. Hashem spent seven days trying to convince Moshe that he was the right person to lead B'nei Yisrael out of the land of Egypt. Hashem was speaking to Moshe; Moshe saw miracles, and yet, he still was not ready to accept the job of leading B'nei Yisrael to freedom. In one exchange, Moshe said, "I am not a man of words—not yesterday, not the day before, and not from the very first time that You spoke to your servant—for I am heavy of mouth and heavy of tongue." The understanding was that Moshe had a speech impediment and that it was difficult for him to speak. This "flaw" gave him pause as to whether he could be the leader that Hashem wanted.

This same fight is one that people in recovery have on a constant basis. The shame and disappointment of being in recovery can cloud their every endeavor. They ask themselves, "Do we deserve what is being given to us? Are we good enough?" And they think, "I can't do that because I'm in recovery. If people actually knew who I was, they would not want to have anything to do with me." Just as Moshe feared that he would not able to lead because of his speech impediment, so too, recovering addicts fear they won't have the ability to flourish due to their past. In reality, this could actually be their greatest strength. Our greatest weakness often becomes our greatest strength.

Moshe, the greatest and most humble leader whom the Jewish people ever have had, almost didn't accept the position. We have to be open to what Hashem has bestowed us with and be willing to take the chance to confront the challenges that are presented to us. The fear, shame, and judgment of ourselves are other manifestations of the addiction. You are worth it and you are capable. Use the struggles that you have endured to lead you to greater heights. Have the confidence!

Va'eira

As you dip your hand into the chip bag for only one chip, it becomes impossible to stop. You can't just stop at one. The one chip becomes eight chips which then becomes the entire bag. That was my delectable experience with the cheesy nacho chips I would eat in college.

In this week's parashah, seven of the ten plagues that Hashem put on the Egyptians are enumerated. The plague of frogs was a unique plague. According to the Torah, "Aharon stretched out his hand over the waters of Egypt, and the frog came up…" What is unusual is that if you read further, the entire Land of Egypt was covered in frogs. According to the Talmud, one frog came out and then a swarm followed. According to the Midrash, there was one large frog that came out of the Nile and the Egyptians kept hitting the frog and more frogs came from the initial frog. The understanding of this Midrash is that the anger that they displayed by striking the frog and then hitting the other frogs gave rise to the swarms of frogs.

Anyone in recovery has heard the saying, "One is too many and a thousand is not enough." That initial frog brought the Egyptian anger out. Then, once they started hitting the frog and all the subsequent frogs, it was out of control. There were frogs in ovens, beds, rooms, etc. The same is true with an addict. Once there is any room for the addiction to enter, it becomes very difficult to get rid of it. The first hit of the substance or action causes a continual desire to continue the actions. Even though the addict sees that his actions are causing chaos, much like the frogs, he doesn't stop. As a matter of fact, he continues to do the same thing, thinking that he will find relief with this action. But, instead of relief, he finds pain, suffering, and confusion. This just leads to a vicious cycle. Unlike the frogs, which stopped after a week, the addict's actions can lead to a lifetime of pain. Just as the Egyptians acquiesced and realized that they were powerless over the frogs and allowed for Hashem to intervene, so an addict needs to realize that he is powerless. Once this first step is taken, then he can start the road to recovery.

Bo

Have you ever been paralyzed by the dark? As a child, did you have a night light or, like yours truly, do you still keep a light on when you sleep in unfamiliar places? Darkness can paralyze us and make us act irrationally, like a child who can't fall asleep because it is dark, and he is terrified of what might be lurking in his closet or hiding under his bed.

In the parashah, we read about the ninth plague, darkness. As noted by *Rashi*, this was no ordinary darkness. This darkness made it so that those who were sitting couldn't stand and those who were standing couldn't sit. It had substance. It terrorized not only the Egyptians, but a portion of the Jewish population as well. According to the Midrash, the darkness was actually Gehinnom, which is known as the place where souls go after death to become purified. It is not the understanding of hell according to other religions, but it is a place of spiritual purification which is not necessarily pleasant.

This darkness, a place of fear and uncertainty, was the experience going on in Egypt. This is similar to the experience that active addicts feel. There is a feeling of despair, uncertainty, fear, and of course, darkness. One feels that there isn't any light that is bright enough to dispel the darkness. Unfortunately, like many of the Egyptians and Jews, many met their death in this darkness. They were never able to leave the darkness or Egypt—much in the same way that one may find himself trapped in the darkness that addiction causes.

Fortunately, as it states in *Yeshayah*, "I form the light and create darkness." Ultimately, Hashem can help shine the light that is necessary to fight the darkness. As it states in Step 4 of the 12 Steps, "Once we have a complete willingness to take inventory, and exert ourselves to do the job thoroughly, a wonderful light falls upon a foggy scene." With the help of programs and integrating spiritual practice, the light that Hashem illuminates upon us will shine forth and allow the darkness to dissipate. As the first Rebbe of the Chabad movement stated, "A little bit of light dispels a lot of darkness."

Beshalach

The word "powerless" means without ability, influence, or power. After B'nei Yisrael went out from Egypt, Pharaoh had a change of heart and pursued them. After experiencing ten plagues over the course of a year, including the death of the firstborn, you would think that the Egyptians, including Pharaoh, would have had enough. Instead, Pharaoh was so anxious to go after B'nei Yisrael that he prepared his own chariot. How can someone who has experienced death, deprivation, and pain go back for more? It seems Pharaoh was powerless over B'nei Yisrael and his hatred for them, and his life was unmanageable.

The Torah teaches us that Pharaoh's heart was hardened by Hashem. How is this possible? Looking at people in active addiction, we know what powerlessness is. We see people who have lost everything yet continue to do the same actions over and over again, putting themselves, their children, and all those around them in harm's way. That is the true act of powerlessness. It makes no logical sense, and it causes death and destruction. That is what addiction is: The act of doing something over and over again, not being able to stop, and progressively spiraling down an abyss.

What logic would make a man put a dirty needle in his leg because he has nowhere else to put the needle, knowing very well that this might be his last time shooting up. Pharaoh was a hardcore addict. He put his family, his friends, and his entire country in jeopardy because he just couldn't stop his addiction: his hatred of the Jews. One might ask if he really had a choice or if he was powerless. As the Torah notes, because Hashem hardened his heart, was it really Pharoah's fault? The answer of course is emphatically: Yes! Pharaoh, like an active addict, gets to the point where he is so desensitized to his actions, that Hashem is no longer aiding him, and he is controlling his decisions. This means that he has pushed Hashem so far from his life that the hardening of his heart was inevitable. But as we see from the Midrash, Pharaoh actually did *teshuvah* and became the ruler in Nineveh. An addict also has the opportunity to bring Hashem back into his life. Then the chaos, the hardening of the heart, and the unmanageability all are put in perspective. If Pharaoh was able to do it, so can we.

Yisro

W hat is that seminal moment in your life—that moment that has stayed frozen in time? That moment that is etched in the minds of everyone who knows you. It is your story, your time, your moment. Sometimes you hear a story from parents or grandparents about their moment and, while listening to the story, it is as if you are there. The story might have such a profound impact on you that it might guide your actions or the way that you see things.

The Ten Commandments are that moment for the Jewish people. There are midrashim that state that every soul from B'nei Yisrael was present at the giving of the Ten Commandments. Every soul experienced this moment, and in turn, there is some residual impact for everyone, thousands of years later. The Ten Commandments defined the Jewish people as a nation with a specific set of laws and guidelines that allowed them to know how to live, and that Hashem was always with them.

For many addicts, the 12 Steps of Alcoholics Anonymous or any recovery program is, *l'havdil*, that set of laws and guidelines for their lives. Before getting into recovery, many have never heard of the 12 Steps of recovery. Even if they had heard of these steps, they didn't necessarily understand how these steps applied to them personally. The same is true for the Ten Commandments. Before receiving the Ten Commandments, there were rules and laws for the Jewish people, but receiving them on Mount Sinai and hearing Hashem give them over directly brought a new reality. There was a mass healing, enthusiasm, and prophecy as a whole which has not been experienced since. So too, the 12 Steps is a set of principles which can guide every aspect of recovery and beyond. Thoughts and actions which an addict might never have considered beforehand are now principles for recovery and living life. Starting with the belief in a higher power and ending with practicing these steps and sharing with other addicts, the 12 Steps, like the Ten Commandments, are able to guide an addict through the moral, emotional, spiritual, and physical challenges that every addict encounters. These 12 Steps are the Ten Commandments of the road to recovery.

Mishpatim

Saying sorry can be one of the most difficult things to do. Sometimes, just paying someone and never needing to make a verbal accounting is easier. Embarrassment and humiliation, along with one's ego, can all inhibit someone from making a verbal restitution.

In the parashah, we are told that, in some instances, a thief needs to pay someone double when he steals: "If the theft shall be found in his hand, whether a live ox or donkey or lamb, he shall pay double." The parashah discusses in great detail about property and the laws dealing with taking something from someone else and also causing damage to another person's property. The idea of paying back what you took and then giving another portion seems fair.

How does an addict ever pay back the people he hurt? As any addict can attest, he has spent a better part of his life hurting other people, damaging their property, or even stealing from them to fuel his addiction. This constant pain and suffering cannot always be paid back by monetary means. Sometimes, there needs to be another way to pay back.

The ninth step of AA states, "Made direct amends to such people wherever possible, except when to do so would injure them or others." Direct amends is not just monetarily paying someone back, but also giving a heartfelt apology to the person. Just as the Torah understands that making remunerations for the exact cost of something is not enough in certain cases, so someone working on his recovery needs to take that added step. Unlike in the Torah, the "double" that one repays in recovery is more severe and much more difficult. Not only does one in recovery need to make restitution where possible or where necessary, he needs to look at the other person face to face, *panim al panim*. Sometimes, these direct amends are the most difficult part of recovery. In reality, this step can lead towards a true healing for the recovering addict and the injured party. And, in many cases, just as King Solomon noted in *Mishlei*, "As in water, face answers to face, so the heart of man to man." The healing and recovery truly begin when the injured party sees that you really are sincere in your attempts to make restitution because it comes from not only from the outside but from the inside as well.

Terumah

Do the clothes make the person or does the person make the clothes? How does having something that is external cause other people to look at us with a greater sense of respect and importance? I remember my first baseball game and not having any idea how to put on my socks. I didn't even hold the glove correctly. That did not make me a baseball player. Years later, as I continued to play baseball, the glove, the glasses, and the cleats each took on a greater significance. Each piece of equipment was dedicated to my one sole passion, to dominate the sport that I loved. The exterior didn't mean much, but instead reflected the work that I did to become a better player.

In *Parashas Terumah*, Hashem tells B'nei Yisrael, "They should make a Sanctuary for Me and I will dwell among them." This famous verse is seen in an important light not so much for Hashem telling B'nei Yisrael to build a Sanctuary for Him, but because He would dwell among them. If Hashem is everywhere, how can Hashem be in one concentrated place more than another? It seems that the Jews needed a place that they could be comfortable connecting with Hashem, as the *Ramban* notes, similar to the experience at Har Sinai. On the other hand, Rabbi Aharon Kotler in *Mishnas Rabbi Aharon* notes that this *pasuk* lets us know that Hashem will dwell within each one of us to different degrees, depending on our actions.

This analogy is similar to the program one creates in sobriety. Many recovering addicts struggle with the Hashem-shaped hole that is within their souls. They are constantly trying to fill it up. Yet, when they start to create a sanctuary of recovery, just as the *Mishkan* was filled with Hashem, so too, is their sanctuary of recovery filled with Hashem. As the recovering addict moves through the process, he gains an entire new outlook on life. Things that never seemed possible are not only possible, but probable. Relationships which were severed are amended, jobs that were unattainable become realistic, and life is completely different. The sanctuary they built becomes filled with light. And just like B'nei Yisrael were told to build the *Mishkan* so that Hashem would dwell amongst them, so too, Hashem walks every step of the way with a person when he is building his sanctuary of recovery. The key is allowing Hashem in and not doing it alone.

Tetzaveh

D id you have siblings or relatives who were always there to remind you of what you should or should not do? When you were just about to start a great game of four-square, he reminded you that it was time to go home for dinner. Or when you were digging into some cake, which you were not supposed to be having at that moment, she would remind you that Mom said no. I know for myself this was so irritating. At times, it could be frustrating, but it was needed because you did not want to remember what you were supposed to do, and that small voice served as a reminder.

In *Parashas Tetzaveh*, we are taught about the Priestly Garments that the Kohen Gadol (High Priest) would wear. These garments bordered on the supernatural, including the *choshen* (breastplate) which had stones that represented each tribe. One garment, the *ephod* (robe), seemed more plain and down to earth. Interestingly enough, the ephod had pomegranate shapes and bells at the bottom. The rabbis explained that the bells were a reminder that the Kohen Gadol was about to enter the most holy chamber on Yom Kippur and that he was to do Hashem's work. The Talmud has another explanation for the bells, that they are a reminder not to speak gossip. Either way, the bells were some sort of reminder.

In recovery, there are not necessarily bells that people wear to remind them of their sobriety and to stay on the path of recovery. There are people who wear rubber bands, strings, necklaces, and other things as a reminder, but there is nothing like the bells that will ring if are about to lose your recovery.

In one program, SAA (Sex Addicts Anonymous), there is a sort of bell that is used and can be used for any form of recovery or just for those who seek to attain balance in their life. This bell is called the circles. The 3 circles consist of an inner, middle, and outer circle. The inner circle are things that one should never do. These are things that do not build us up, but instead tear us down. So, for example, an alcoholic can never drink. The middle circle is a warning system that lets you know you could be in danger. For example, for an alcoholic, it might be walking into a bar or being at a party where everyone is drunk. The outer circle are behaviors that lead one to health, stability, gratitude, happiness, and strength. For example, writing, reading a book, praying, spending time with someone who makes you happy, going to the beach, and the list goes on and on. The circles, or bells, are a sign to help lead you back to the path of sobriety. Just as the bells were a signal for the High Priest, so too the circles are a signal for all of us.

Ki Sisa

Have you ever felt really down on yourself? You made some sort of mistake or mistakes and have no idea how you can forgive yourself. Perhaps, you even continue making similar mistakes. Of course, this sounds a lot like addiction: the inability to stop doing something that you know that you need to stop doing, but you just can't do it. Most addicts who grew up with any form of religion have a double-edged sword. The concept of Hashem, which they bring with them into recovery, can be a blessing or, it can start to tear at the fabric of their foundation. It might make them think things like: They're no good, Hashem hates them, or that Hashem is going to punish them for every mistake that they make. Likewise, every misfortune that they experience becomes an admonition from Hashem, creating a vicious cycle. It's like there is a stern parent or an angry teacher punishing them, judging them, and wanting to make their life miserable.

In the parashah, we see an interesting assortment when it comes to the incense offering. The different ingredients for the incense are mentioned. As the list is mentioned, there is one ingredient which does not seem to fit. Galbanum, which is also used for digestive issues and other medicinal purposes, is not a particularly nice smelling herb. Since the incense was supposed to have a pleasing smell, why add a disgusting smelling herb? The Talmud (*Kerisos* 6b) teaches that Galbanum was included to illustrate that all Jews are included when it comes to serving Hashem. The Sages understood that some people felt that they should not be included, but the lesson of the incense teaches us that everyone is included, regardless of his "smell." Not only that, the incense cannot be offered unless all of the prescribed ingredients are present, so, despite its awful smell, the Galbanum has to be there; it's essential.

This is a concept that recovering addicts must come to realize and appreciate, especially those that come from a religious or spiritual background. They come to turn to Hashem, and in Step 3, turn their will and their lives over to the care of Hashem as they understand Him. Through this understanding, they can come to a place where they accept that Hashem loves them and that they are not uniquely awful. They can let go of the idea that Hashem is angry with them or dislikes them because their actions are so abhorrent. Instead, they remain a part of the larger community. Yes, we are responsible for our actions, and there are consequences for things that we do, but at the same time, we have a partner in this struggle: Hashem. The same Hashem who they used to fear, hate, and feel despondent about now becomes a partner, ready to help as they courageously work the steps. So, the next time you know someone who feels that he is beyond repair or that Hashem doesn't want him, remind him about the incense offering. It lets us know that Hashem loves us and wants us to be a part of His community. This makes the road to recovery so much more manageable.

Vayakhel

We have all heard the famous adage not to judge a book by its cover. Yet, we live in a physical world where it is impossible not to get caught up in appearances and other physical entrapments, such as what kind of car someone drives, what kind of house he lives in, and what kind of family he comes from. All these factors can go into determining what we think of someone. How can a doctor be driving an old, beat-up car? Is she humble or is she just not a very good doctor?

In *Parashas Vayakhel*, Hashem puts Betzalel and Oholiav in charge of the craftsmanship of the *Mishkan*, the portable temple in the desert. The Torah mentions that Oholiav was from the tribe of Dan, which was one of the lowest of the tribes, whereas Betzalel was from the tribe of Yehudah, which was one of the greatest tribes. They each were imbued with "the spirit of Hashem, wisdom, and insight…" *Rashi* teaches us that Hashem put them on equal footing. The previous Lubavitcher Rebbe teaches us that this encouraged everyone, poor and rich alike, to see his contribution as meaningful. Each person felt that he had a purpose and meaning and that his contributions were significant.

Early on, recovering addicts learn that they should try to get a sponsor, someone who can help guide them as they face the struggles of recovery. They realize that a guide is an important tool that can help shape the way that they work the steps and approach recovery. Just as Oholiav was imbued with wisdom from Hashem, so too, the sponsor, *l'havdil*, is imbued with the strength and ability to guide the recovering addict. A sponsor is someone who has worked the steps successfully and has demonstrated the ability to stay sober. There are no prerequisites regarding which kind of car he drives, where he lives, or what kind of job he has. Needless to say, a sponsor might have been homeless, destitute, divorced, separated from his family, incarcerated, or unemployed. None of these things matter, nor does the sex, race, religion, or ethnicity of the sponsor. Instead, it is the wisdom with which Hashem imbued him that guides his leadership. This is how you can have an African-American, Southern Baptist car mechanic sponsoring a chareidi rabbi from Monsey. The identifiable traits that every sponsor needs to have are stated clearly in the Serenity Prayer: "Hashem grant me the **serenity** to accept the things that I cannot change, the **courage** to change the things that I can, and the **wisdom** to know the difference." Serenity, courage, and wisdom are three important tools that sponsors use to help others. Just as Hashem imbued Oholiav and Betzalel with a spirit of wisdom, insight, and G-dliness, these are the tools, *l'havdil*, with which Hashem imbues a sponsor in order to help him lead those who need support and guidance.

Pekudei

I remember as a child when I was asked to clean my room by my parents. It was annoying, and I pushed back before reluctantly cleaning my room. As a matter of fact, I even made sure to vacuum and even dust around my favorite toys. I felt pretty proud of myself and then the ultimate blow came.My parents said, "Great, now go help your sister with her room, bringing with it feelings of disappointment, anger, and annoyance for having to go and help my sibling do the very thing that I had just done by myself.

In *Parashas Pekudei*, Moshe is asked by Hashem to erect the *Mishkan*, the portable tabernacle, for the Jewish people. He was told where the items went in the *Mishkan* and the day that it should be erected. The Previous Lubavitcher Rebbe explains that Moshe already had his own personal tabernacle, the *Ohel Mo'ed* (the Tent of Meeting), so why did he need to help the B'nei Yisrael erect their tabernacle? Rabbi Schneerson answers that it is because someone cannot only look after his own needs, especially spiritually, but should be concerned to help others.

In the recovery world this is affectionately known as Step 12, which is when one has a spiritual awakening. "Step 12 requires you to have a spiritual awakening that came as a result of completing the previous 11 steps, carry the message to other addicts, and practice the principles of the program in all of your daily affairs." One who has worked so hard to stop an addiction that maybe he has struggled with for a large portion of his life, is not told to ride off into the sunset and bask in his accomplishments. Instead, he is told to give to other people, to help those who are still struggling with addiction and in need of recovery on their spiritual journey to sobriety. We need to understand that we are not merely individuals, but that we are part of a greater community, with a responsibility to go out and help others on their journey. Just as Moshe was told by Hashem to guide B'nei Yisrael in setting up their place of worship even though his was already set, so too, anyone who has worked the 12 Steps of recovery is obligated to go support those who are still on the road to building their personal tabernacle and in search of their spiritual connection and sobriety.

Vayikra

I can't forget sitting in the pep rally during high school and listening as the entire football team was introduced. As they went through the starting lineup, when they finally got to the star quarterback, there was a mini parade. The accolades didn't stop coming. Everyone cheered and the adornment didn't end with the pep rally. Instead, as he walked in the hallways, there was an idol worship of sorts. The looks, glances, and entitlement that went with holding that position were unparalleled.

In *Parashas Vayikra*, the very first word, "*Vayikra*," is written with a small *alef*. This is very notable, so, of course, this causes the rabbis to ask the question: Why is there a small *alef*? The *Pane'ach Raza*, written by the fourth-century rabbi, Yitzchak ben Yehudah, states that the *alef* was small to signify the humility of Moshe. Since Moshe spoke with Hashem on a regular basis, it would not be shocking if he had developed an ego, especially in front of the Jewish people. On the contrary, Moshe was known as the humblest person. Even with all of his accolades and importance, Moshe still was able to check his ego and see his place in the scope of humanity.

Humility allows one to be devoid of pride and not to see himself as more than he is. I would argue that for someone to walk into a 12-Step room takes humility. To go a step further, to tell a room full of people your faults, your most intimate details, and admit defeat takes courage and humility. To fully embrace sobriety, one has to become like Moshe. The unchecked ego was partly responsible for the continued life that was filled with cheating, telling untruths, and displaying a false sense of who a person is. One has to shed his ego, look in the mirror, and accept responsibility for his actions. The first step, admitting powerlessness, is not something that we embrace in our culture. We often feel that we have to always have a plan, a witty response, and proof that we are in control. But what if that is not true? What if, instead, we are able to cede that control to a supernatural Being who we can't see, hear, feel, or smell? What if we realize that being humble means that we don't have all the answers? Once we accept that, then we can start on the road to recovery.

Tzav

I remember playing with my friends and throwing the ball that broke my neighbor's window. I felt terrible for the mistake and wanted to make amends. The only problem was that, once the neighbor found out, the entire neighborhood found out about it. Every adult that saw me reminded me of my infraction and made sure I knew that I may not throw a ball anywhere near his house. The embarrassment and shame I felt was palpable. I made a mistake, said I was sorry, used my allowance to help buy a new window, and was ready to move forward.

In *Parashat Tzav*, we see that when one offered an *olah* (burnt) offering, which was for sins of thoughts that were not so pure, it was brought where the *chatas* (sin) offering was performed. On the other hand, a *chatas* offering was brought for much more serious sins. It seems perplexing that two offerings for completely different categories of sins were brought in the same place. The *Kli Yakar*, a commentary by the sage Rabbi Shlomo Ephraim Luntschitz, notes that the two offerings were brought in the same place on purpose. It was to ease the shame of the person who was bringing the more serious offering. Since no one knew which offering a person was bringing, people would be more willing to bring the offering for the more serious sin.

So it is with sobriety. Everyone who comes into the room of a 12-Step program and seeks recovery has his own story. No two stories are alike. Each person brings his own history and shame. When we walk into the rooms, that shame should dissipate. No one is better or worse in those rooms. It is truly an egalitarian atmosphere. Everyone is coming from a place of improvement. Each person wants sobriety and all the work that that entails. There are some things that people did that are more extreme than what other people did, but no one in the meeting is judging. No one even cares. Instead, everyone is bringing his own offering, working his own path to sobriety, and ultimately, making amends with whomever or wherever he needs to make them. This path is guided by the principles of the 12 Steps and the guiding light, focusing on progress, not perfection. Just as a sinner during the Temple times needed to feel safe to bring an offering, so too, does an addict need a place to feel safe and work on his recovery without the constant judgment and shame that he might feel outside that room.

Shemini

Have you ever known that person who is Mr. Gregarious in one realm and a complete jerk in another? He turns on the charm when he needs to and, behind closed doors, he is someone else? He receives all kinds of accolades and then you find out it was all a facade.

In *Parashas Shemini*, we find the laws about which animals are kosher and which animals are not, based upon certain signs. For example, a fish needs scales and fins. When it comes to domesticated animals, they need to chew the cud and have completely split hooves. There are only four animals that the Torah names that have one of these two signs, but not both or neither. Of these four, only the pig has completely split hooves but does not chew its cud. According to Rav Moshe Mordechai Epstein, these two signs represent, on the one hand, what we show people on the outside, the split hooves, and on the other hand, who we really are on the inside, chewing one's cud. The pig is vilified for representing the outward projection of appearing to be something that it truly is not.

Many addicts fall into this category. They are the award winners, the life of the party, the overachievers, the people with the amazing exterior. On the inside, there is a very different story. There is the wife of 25 years who finds out her husband was a serial cheater. A husband of 15 years finds out that his soccer mom wife is abusing opioids. There is the revered rebbi who struggles with inappropriate materials. They struggle to keep it together regarding the outside world and even, at times, to keep it together in front of those closest to them—until they don't, until their true colors eventually come out. Like any animal that is clearly kosher or non-kosher, these behaviors are true to themselves. The struggle of recovery is accepting that we might not chew our cud or have split hooves, so to speak.

Part of the road to recovery is understanding who we are, accepting ourselves, and having a willingness to realize that we are powerless over our addiction. Once we do that, we stop trying to be something that we are not. Instead of sitting like a pig, which looks one way but is really something else, we start the road to recovery by ending the charade.

Tazria

I remember as a child being sent to my room and being asked to think about whatever thing that I had done wrong. It might have been a fight with a sibling, the way I spoke to my parents, or some other form of mischievous behavior for which I was being punished. The time was meant for reflection. Today, children are often told to go to a safe space to reflect. Regardless of what it is called, the idea is that there is some reflection and that, when the time is over, the child comes back more resilient and ready to not make the same mistakes again.

In *Tazria*, we see that there is a time out or safe space to which the person who is afflicted with *tzaraas* (some sort of spiritual malady manifesting itself, among other things, as a skin disease) goes. The Torah notes that the person is isolated for a week and then, depending on what is found, he may need to continue to stay isolated. In *Vayikra* (13:46) it notes, "So long as the lesion is upon them, one will be ritually impure. One should remain isolated. Their place is outside the camp." According to the *Rambam*, the isolation is to teach the lesson that the person should stop speaking in a derogatory manner about others. *Rashi* also notes that it is important for one to think about his speech. Even though this is a punishment, this time away is really more for self-reflection and inner peace. The ability to work on difficult things is, quite frankly, difficult. When surrounded by the same temptation, it makes it that much more difficult.

The recovering addict often needs to separate himself from his community as well. The difficulty of staying in the same place where he struggled with his addictive behaviors is one fraught with failure. Just as one who is afflicted with *tzaraas* will find it difficult not to gossip when surrounded by the very people that he either spoke gossip about or to whom he spoke gossip, the recovering addict often needs to change his scenery as he is working on his recovery. Often specific places, people, or situations will lead him down that dark road again.

For some people, this means that they need to go to an in-patient treatment center, where they can live for an extended period of time, so that they can clearly focus on their recovery without the day-to-day distractions that might otherwise hold them back. For others, this will include an outpatient treatment option, which will allow them to work on their treatment while then going home or staying in a hotel while they are focusing on their recovery. Other recovering addicts do not need either of these options, but instead go to 12-Step meetings, talk to a therapist or a coach, get a sponsor, and change certain routines and habits which led them down their difficult path. The idea of being isolated is one which allows an addict to contemplate what got him to this point in his life and what he can do to change his current circumstances. And, just like the loving parent, these options of isolation are not meant to punish per say, but instead intended to change the behavior and lead one towards a more fulfilled life.

Metzora

I remember as a child hiding fun things in my backyard. My friends and I loved digging in the dirt and burying cool toys to find later. Sometimes, you would lose the toys and then on a random day when you were looking for something else, lo and behold, you would find a hidden treasure. We were so elated, and it was truly unexpected.

In *Parashas Metzora,* we learn the laws of *tzaraas,* a biblical disease that could afflict the body, clothing, vessels or even one's house. If *tzaraas* was found in a house, the owner needed to tell a Kohen, so that he could come and inspect the house. After checking several times, if the *tzaraas* had spread, the house was demolished. What an awful punishment for this affliction. According to the Midrash, however, these lesions ended up being something positive for B'nei Yisrael, because even though their house was destroyed, they often found hidden treasures in the walls. These treasures had been left behind by the previous occupants, who had decided to abandon their houses. This hidden treasure far outweighed the destruction of the house. Without the impending destruction, the treasure never would have been found.

This is no different from a recovering addict. Many times, an addict needs to hit bottom before he can get sober. The idea of hitting bottom is one where one cannot go any lower than he already is. This might include things like divorce, loss of a job, incarceration, or any number of awful consequences. At the time, the addict feels that these consequences are just another punishment from Hashem—a way for Hashem to continue to hurt him. Yet, once the addict becomes sober, he realizes that it is Hashem's love that brought him to such a low point. For if he had not hit bottom, he would never have become sober or, even worse, he might have ended up dead. The treasure that the addict finds is sobriety. This treasure can help build a new improved life from the swath of destruction that his life incurred through his path of using. Just as B'nei Yisrael were unable to see the hidden treasures that were waiting for them in the houses into which they moved, and had to go through some difficulty for these treasures to be revealed to them, so too, an addict needs to experience the destruction of his current house to find the treasure hidden within.

Acharei Mos

I'm sorry. I'm sorry. Really, how many times can you hear this? Growing up, I remember loaning my cassette tapes to my sister and constantly being disappointed because I rarely got them back. She'd say sorry and then do the same thing over and over again. It's natural that we don't want someone apologizing for the same thing again and again. Instead, make a mistake, sincerely regret it, apologize, and move on. Yet, this is contrary to how Hashem works.

In *Parashas Acharei Mos*, we learn about Yom Kippur. We are told, "In the seventh month, on the tenth day of the month...For on this day (Hashem) will atone for you, to cleanse you. You will be cleansed from all your sins before Hashem." According to one opinion in the *Talmud*, (*Yoma* 85b) one receives atonement if he does *teshuvah* on Yom Kippur. According to the *Rambam*, one receives atonement on Yom Kippur, but it's only effective if one feels genuine remorse. This is an interesting outlook on repentance, especially for addicts. Many addicts feel that they have made so many mistakes that they can no longer be forgiven. They compound these mistakes with more mistakes because they feel so badly about the past that they feel there is no use in trying to improve. They think things such as: I've already cheated on my wife, or lost my house because of gambling issues, or my children won't talk to me because of my continual benders, or whatever it might be. This short-sighted thinking is what helps get them into their predicament in the first place. Realizing both that they are powerless and that there is a higher power is integral to finding recovery. Hashem is not a man. Hashem does forgive. The Torah clearly states that we can be forgiven for our sins. If we are sorry for our actions and we make a choice to go down a different path, there is a forgiveness process. Granted, it is different for sins between people and Hashem versus sins between people. No matter the addiction, there is a possibility of redemption. The process of recovery involves forgiving oneself and then seeking forgiveness. Working the 12 Steps helps to start the recovery process. We need to look at ourselves in the mirror, admit our faults, and put one foot forward, taking one step at a time. The Torah is filled with stories of things that many people could never imagine doing, yet there is a process for forgiveness. The recovering addict needs to realize that there is a process to recovery and that, ultimately, through this process, he will find that not only will Hashem forgive him, but—while working the steps—others who he has hurt along the way will also forgive him.

Kedoshim

Did you ever have an awkward neighbor who moved in when you were a child? Your parents asked you to go over to his house, introduce yourself, invite him over for a playdate to befriend him. It felt uncomfortable and unnatural. Why was your mom forcing you to befriend somebody who seemed so different from you and try to develop a friendship in a way that maybe none of your other friendships occurred?

In *Parashas Kedoshim*, it seems that Hashem is asking us to do the exact same thing. "You should love your fellow as you love yourself. I am Hashem" (*Vayikra* 19:18). The commentaries ask a lot of questions on this verse. It seems difficult and unnatural to love someone as you love yourself. Is this for everyone, some people, or just Jews? Rabbi Akiva says that this verse is a major principle of the Torah. Two other major commentators note that it is impossible to love another as you love yourself, but its purpose is for us to show love for others by respecting their property and by assisting them.

This ties right into Step 12 of Alcoholics Anonymous. "Having had a spiritual awakening as the result of these steps, we tried to carry this message to alcoholics, and to practice these principles in all our affairs." Step 12 is all about being of service and giving back to other people. For anyone who has been in a 12-Step meeting, he knows that one of the miracles of such a meeting is the way that people whom you have never met or seen before come up to you and offer to help. Do you need a call? Did you need to talk? Do you want to go to lunch? Do you need a ride? A myriad of questions can pepper a newcomer as he walks into the room for his first meeting. He might even feel overwhelmed by this show of love and support from so many people whom he doesn't even know.

Why do these people care about you when you, at that very moment, might be loathing yourself? This principle of "love your neighbor like yourself" flows through the very essence of the 12 Steps. As every recovering addict knows, a person does not become sober by himself. Instead, it takes help from other people. It is almost a "pay it forward" aspect of the program which perpetuates the acts of lovingkindness which run through the veins of all those who are sober. Loving your neighbor might be a way for people to give back and show gratitude for whatever blessings are in their life at the moment. And, for a recovering addict, there is also one blessing, sobriety, that he has and is willing to share.

Emor

As a child, I remember watching my favorite sports team and thinking that I could make a difference in the outcome. If I cheered enough, wore a certain pair of socks, or didn't watch, these things would all have an effect on the outcome of the game. Ultimately, whether I watched, cheered, wore my favorite jersey, or did none of the above, the outcome was inconsequential to my actions. I had no control over the grown men playing a sport; I was just an observer.

In the parashah, we are asked to sanctify Hashem's name by not desecrating Hashem's name. "You should not desecrate My Holy Name; it should be sanctified…" The Rabbis discuss: If someone makes the decision to give up his life to sanctify Hashem's name, will he be saved or will he lose his life? *Rashi*, the *Rambam*, and even more contemporary commentators such as the previous Lubavitcher Rebbe, among others, discuss this point. Obviously, there are ways to sanctify Hashem's name other than by dying for Hashem's name.

One can make the case that one sanctifies Hashem's name by doing a myriad of actions. One example is through Step 3 of any 12-Step program: "Make a decision to turn our will and our lives over to the care of Hashem as we understood Him." This is one way that recovering addicts sanctify Hashem's name. Since many addicts have no relationship with a Higher Power or they come from an environment where Hashem is to be feared but there is no love, turning over their will to a Higher Power is an act of sanctification. Their complex and convoluted relationship with Hashem is magnified by their addiction, which just compounds their self-loathing and, in turn, distances them from Hashem. To have faith and trust that their affliction can actually be taken away by a Higher Power is reminiscent of *Rashi*'s understanding of the *pasuk*, "Surrender yourself and sanctify My Name…when the person surrenders himself, he should be prepared to die…"

The recovering addict was at the precipice many times, at the intersection of life and death, which is why he is now in recovery. Having the willingness to believe that a Higher Power can actually save you means that you are essentially willing to die, as the fear of the unknown is so great that using seems like the only alternative. Believing in something greater than yourself is a true leap of faith. A recovering addict has faith that this elusive Higher Power is there for him and ready and willing to help him whenever he's ready for help. And it is true. So, what does this have to do with sports and rooting for your favorite team? Unlike a child who has faith that his favorite sports team is going to win or lose based on his actions, Hashem really is there to help, while your favorite socks or chair have no outcome on the game.

Behar

It is so difficult to give of yourself without wanting or expecting anything in return. Being truly altruistic takes practice. We are not born with the ability to give and not receive. There is always that little part of you that wants recognition, a small reward, or to receive some sort of benefit. Even when it comes to mitzvos, there is only one mitzvah that is seen as being purely about giving without any desire to receive something back, and that is burying the dead. In *Parashas Behar*, we are asked not to loan money on interest. "...help your fellow man to live with you. You should not lend him money with interest, nor food..."

According to the *Sefer Hachinuch*, an anonymous thirteenth-century halachic work, the reason that we are urged to loan money without interest is to help us develop the attributes of compassion, kindness, and empathy. These are lofty goals, but do we really see people giving so altruistically in day-to-day life?

I think of the idea of brother/sisterhood that happens for those in the 12-Step program. Step 12 is all about giving, without expecting anything in return. This step requires you to have a spiritual awakening that comes as a result of completing the previous 11 steps, carry the message to other addicts, and practice the principles of the twelve steps in all of your daily affairs. By carrying the message, you can walk into any 12-Step room anywhere in the world and find someone who is willing to listen to you, spend time with you, go out for a meal, give you a ride, and be a genuine support while expecting nothing in return. Rabbi Dr. Twersky, who helped mainstream the 12 Steps within the traditional Jewish community, tells a story about how amazed he was when he realized that you could call someone in the program at 2:00 a.m. and that person would pick up. He understood that this type of altruism was not necessarily present in regular Jewish life. This sort of devotion and caring for another is part of all 12-Step programs. So, even though it is not easy, we can see that we can loan without interest and, in turn, give of ourselves without expecting anything in return.

Bechukosai

D o remember when you were a child and your parents told you not to do something? They then would go and give you consequences for your actions. One temptation that every child experiences is the desire to eat treats and sweets all the time. Your parents might very well tell you that it isn't healthy, that too many sweets might cause diabetes, obesity, or have other side effects. It is not that your parents are going to punish you directly, but these are the consequences of your actions.

In *Parashas Bechukosai*, Hashem explicitly states that the Jewish people will have consequences for not observing the commandments. Famine, war, captivity, death, expulsion, and the destruction of the Temple are some of the very harsh consequences that are laid out if the Jewish people do not follow the commandments according to the parashah. As noted, these seem to be consequences from Hashem, not punishments.

This is similar to what happens when one is struggling with his addiction. He might feel that he is being targeted or punished by those around him, including greater society. Loss of a job, a spouse, incarceration, monetary instability, disease, and depression are a few of the consequences that one might encounter while struggling with active addiction. But the addict needs to see that these are not punishments, but consequences. No one is doing this to the addict. The addict is suffering from the consequences of his actions.

So too, in the parashah, Hashem is not necessarily punishing us, but letting us know that the mitzvos are the antidote for what ails us. Likewise, sobriety is the antidote for what ails us. The consequences, or so-called punishments, cease to exist once we clear the wreckage of our past. Once one follows the path towards sobriety, Hashem is there to lend a helping hand, and the blessings that come with sobriety will soon follow. The past and the struggles of the past will not necessarily disappear, but those unintended consequences of our actions will. Instead of walking down a desolate path filled with proverbial minefields, we are left with a path that is best suited for recovery and one in which life seems a bit more manageable.

Bamidbar

I remember playing baseball for the first time. I had no idea what I was doing. In my very first time at bat in my very first game, I stood over the plate, swinging down as if I was chopping a tree. I still remember the umpire picking up my 32-pound body and placing me on the side of the plate so I could swing. Fortunately, through a lot of training, practice, and coaching, I learned to play baseball.

In *Parashas Bamidbar*, there is a *pasuk* (*Bamidbar* 3:1) which states that these are the names of Aharon's and Moshe's children. Reading further, however, we find that the *pasuk* only mentions the names of the children of Aharon, but not Moshe. We know that Moshe taught Aharon's children. Based on this *pasuk*, the Rabbi's teach (*Sanhedrin* 19b) that one who teaches another person's son Torah, it is as if he gave birth to him. The understanding is that by giving someone spiritual nourishment, you are virtually creating a new soul.

This parallel is very similar to the sponsor/sponsee relationship. When someone walks into a 12-Step meeting for the very first time, he is almost like a newborn. Unsure of where to go, not sure what to do, and having no idea how to move forward. Within the space of a 12-Step meeting, one gets a sense of understanding and, in turn, how he can move his life forward. This sense is helped by the guidance of a sponsor. The sponsor becomes the recovering addict's go-to person, his mentor. The sponsor might work with him on not only how to stay away from alcohol or drugs, but also how to go to bed at night and get up in the morning.

Many times, a recovering addict needs to reprogram his entire being to help as he moves forward in his road towards recovery. Just as a coach guides someone in a sport or a teacher helps imbue morals and values into a student's soul, so too does a sponsor help guide a new birth and a new awakening for the recovering addict. The righteousness of a sponsor is similar to a parent, as sponsors tend to be the person willing to listen, receive phone calls at any time of the day, and show up when the sponsee has a crisis. Receiving a phone call at 2:00 a.m., which might seem insane to anyone other than a parent or a spouse, is simply a part of the love and guidance that a sponsor shows.

So no, Moshe did not birth Aharon's children, but he helped to imbue within them a sense of love, commitment, and understanding as they took their positions within the Jewish nation. And my coach did not go to bat for me as I learned to hit right and left-handed. So, a sponsor becomes a friend, a companion, and an alternate parent as he helps a recovering addict on his journey through his own desert, moving from struggle to freedom.

Naso

I n *Parashas Naso*, we read the story of the *nazir*. The *nazir* is somebody who would voluntarily refrain from going near a dead body, cutting his hair and beard, and having any wine or grape products whatsoever. The verse about the *nazir* states, "A man or woman shall disassociate himself by taking a nazirite vow," and then later on in the Hebrew it uses the word *"yafli"* which means to separate oneself. The *Ibn Ezra*, a Spanish commentator from the Middle Ages, says that this word connects to the word *pele*. The word *pele* means something wondrous. The connection here is that it was seen as wondrous that one would voluntarily take a vow not to eat a particular item. We know that the *nazir* was not even allowed so much as the skin of a grape. He had to refrain completely from anything that has to do with grapes and grape products.

There is an obvious connection between this type of separation and abstinence from drinking and recovery. One knows that when he is working towards recovery, whether it's with alcohol, drugs, sex, gambling, food, or any other addiction, he must work very hard to abstain from those actions which caused chaos in his life. He has to follow a similar sort of path to the *nazir* by refraining from all these things. When one wants recovery, he also makes a sort of vow. For example, if one is struggling with alcohol, he knows that he cannot drink anymore. If one is struggling with marijuana use, he knows that he can't smoke marijuana anymore. If one is struggling from sex addiction, he might have to take himself away from inappropriate materials and situations.

Anyone who has struggled with addictive qualities in his life knows that it's very difficult to give things up. The chocolate chip cookie, a glass of wine, or anything else that seems so tempting is almost impossible to leave behind and is similar to what the *nazir* gives up. Someone suffering from addiction almost needs to take a similar vow to the *nazir* that he will not go anywhere near whatever it is that he is struggling with. Just like a *nazir*, who is unable to drink wine or go anywhere near grape products while the rest of society remains able to do so, the same is true for somebody who is struggling with addiction.

They may have to stop going to the bar when their friends are going. Maybe they have to order differently and can't eat the exact same food that everyone else is eating. Maybe they can't watch certain movies that everybody else seems to be able to watch. To the outside world this might seem strange, and people might ask questions as to why someone would choose to do this. But, as was the case with a *nazir*, one has to look at this recovery as a *pele*, a wonder. This wonder is almost an open miracle. Just as a *nazir* knows that this is what he needs to move forward in his spiritual connection to Hashem, so too does a recovering addict know that he has to take certain steps to live his life in a healthy manner and to reignite his spiritual connection to a higher power. May everyone merit the strength and the open miracle that he needs in order to move forward with his sustained recovery.

Behaalosecha

Responsibility is not an easy thing to deal with. In *Parashas Behaalosecha*, the Jewish people again complain to Moshe about the *mohn* and seem to forget about their slavery when they were in Egypt (*Bamidbar* 11:4). They were very upset, and they reminded Moshe about all the delicacies that they had in Egypt which included leeks, onions, cucumbers, watermelon, and garlic. Rather surprisingly, they claimed that they had received all of these things for free. That slaves would receive all these things for free does not make sense and there are many explanations as to what they were talking about when they said that they were free.

There is a deeper way of looking at this episode when we connect it with the 12 Steps of recovery. *Rashi* teaches that when the Jews said that they received these things for free, they meant that they didn't have to do mitzvos. Once they left Egypt and received the Ten Commandments, however, everything changed. Once we received the Torah, then there was a commitment and expectation. Up to this point, there was no commitment between the Jewish people and Hashem.

In general, the Jews did not have any Torah and mitzvos responsibility in Egypt. I think that this is what happens to recovering addicts. They see themselves and their inability to get sober, and they don't want to do the work that must be done to get sober. The work is very challenging, difficult, and time-consuming. It will change everything, and they will miss out on things. They actually say things like: "I remember when I could drink without impunity; I could take drugs without impunity; I could be intimate with whomever I wanted, whenever I wanted and it didn't matter. Everything was a lot less tense. I could just do what I wanted. I didn't have to struggle. Now, I have to go to meetings. Before, I didn't have to account to anybody, and I didn't have to necessarily account to a Higher Power, and it was easier." Just like the Jewish people in Egypt, despite the fact that they were slaves, they didn't have that responsibility of fulfilling Torah and mitzvos, so in that respect it was easier for them.

I think that what the verses are teaching us is that this responsibility takes time. It doesn't just happen overnight, and you have to work it just like a program. The ability for a person to receive the Torah is akin to the ability for someone to achieve sobriety. A person has to be able to open up and to forget about his "freedom", so to speak. His freedom to drink, smoke, be lustful, eat what he wants, or whatever else it might be with which he's struggling. Deep down, an addict knows that those things were not really free, and he paid a steep price for them, just as the Jews paid a steep price for the watermelon, cucumbers, and fresh fish that they received.

Let's say that the Jews did get these things to eat while they were slaves. None of it was free. They were desperately and strenuously working, with many Jews dying and most Jews suffering tremendous hardships. During the years of slavery, they didn't really have an identity or connections with their Higher Power until they saw the miracles that took place, were taken out of Egypt, and crossed the Yam Suf. It's the same thing with recovery. Not until someone actually does the work do they realize that their prior irresponsible actions really came at a very high cost. That cost could be in relationships, jobs, and their mental, emotional, or spiritual health. None of it came for free. Yes, it may have come without responsibility, but that's not freedom. It was its own servitude. One has to remember that walking away from servitude doesn't mean that freedom will be easy and that everything is going to be fine. Freedom takes time, effort, and energy. Only with that time, effort, and energy is one able to have true freedom, the freedom that allows you to be sober and to live your life without servitude. Just as the Jews were servants and slaves in Egypt, so too, addicts are servants and slaves to their addiction. If the addict can realize that nothing was free, he can then recognize the lack of personal responsibility which came with a heavy cost, and only then can he move forward.

Shelach

How many times have we been ready to give up? We are frustrated with our spouse, our living situation, our job, our pain, our financial situation, or a myriad of other issues. We look in the mirror and question: What is the point? We feel that we are just spinning our wheels.

In *Parashas Shelach*, B'nei Yisrael were told that it will be another forty years until they would be brought to Eretz Yisrael. They were also told that most of them were going to die in the desert and never make it to Eretz Yisrael. So, one might ask, what is the point? Why do I need to go on? Why should I continue to do mitzvos? This is a relevant question that is answered by Tzelophechad, as he was caught carrying wood on Shabbos, which is one of the thirty-nine forbidden labors. Ultimately, he was taken out and killed. According to *Tosafos*, this happened in order to teach the Jewish people that they were still responsible for keeping the Torah and mitzvos. Otherwise, they might have thought that since they were not going to enter Eretz Yisrael anyway, they did not need to keep the mitzvos.

This is similar to a recovering addict who continues to relapse. Every relapse brings the recovering addict closer to his own personal abyss. There is a feeling that he will never be able to recover from his addictions. This leads him to continue to use because, ultimately, his actions don't matter to him. He feels helpless. He feels that his family, friends, and the world have given up on him. This, of course, is not true. Once one is in recovery, he will always be in recovery. It does not mean that he has to continue the actions, but it does mean that he will continually work on his program. It also lets us know that Hashem is always there for us. Our actions are always important, and we should never give up faith or hope. Instead, one should attack each day, one day at a time, with fervor and importance. If we get caught up in the past, we lose the relevancy of today.

It's been said that if we have one leg in yesterday and one in tomorrow, we make a mess of today. We should know that we are important, our actions are relevant, and, regardless of what happened in the past, even moments ago, we still can make the present moment important and worthwhile. We should not dwell on what happened or what we did. Instead, we should focus on our current actions. Just as in the case of the one who was punished for breaking the laws of Shabbos which was done to teach us the importance of our present actions, so too, we can apply that same lesson elsewhere in our lives and see that all is not lost. We can always create meaning in our present actions. We always have a place and relevance in Hashem's universe.

Korach

Do you remember when you were a child and you got your hand caught in the cookie jar? Your parents asked what you were doing and, somehow, you concocted a lie about what happened. You then proceeded to add a lie to what you had already done and then you made a scene. You didn't stop at one transgression but continued to add one thing onto another. Before you knew it, you had gotten in way over your head and didn't see a way out. At this point, your focus becomes sheer survival. What started as a simple taking of a cookie ends up becoming a federal case, where you now find yourself grounded for two weeks, having pulled in multiple family members and gone to a place that you never thought you would go.

Korach had a similar situation as he went from a place of prosperity and prominence to death and destruction. He never could have realized that his actions would get him a one-way ticket to purgatory according to the Talmud, being swallowed by a hole in the earth. All of this was because he saw himself with greater prominence than he really deserved. Korach's stubbornness and jealousy led him to unprecedented depths in the Torah. The pain and suffering that he caused not only impacted him, but his family, the tribe of Reuven, and, in turn, all of Yisrael.

This pain and torment because of stubbornness and not calculating the depths of one's actions is seen in active addicts. They set their focus on whatever it is that they want to attain, but they are sometimes so shortsighted that they can't comprehend the depth of the pain that their actions will cause. They also become so immersed in their addiction that, just as Korach did, they go to depths that never seemed imaginable. This can lead to divorce, incarceration, bankruptcy, diseases, and even death. Their sole focus becomes their obsession, and they find any pretext to get what they think they want. Unfortunately, just as Korach was fooled into thinking that he knew what was best, those in active addiction "know" what's best when, in reality, their actions speak otherwise. We can learn from Korach's one-sidedness that a more thoughtful, balanced approach is the way to go. When one becomes so immersed in something that he knows is right, he forgets the purpose of what he is doing. As with Korach, it can have life altering effects.

Chukas

In one of the strangest commandments of the Torah, *Parashas Chukas* starts with the description of the *parah adumah*, whereby ashes of a completely red heifer are placed on someone who is ritually impure in order to purify him. What makes this truly unusual is that, while the impure person becomes pure through the ashes, the people involved with the preparation of the ashes become impure. This is one of the mitzvos, commandments, that are called a *chok* (a law that is not rationally understandable). Whereas the commandment to not murder or steal make rational sense, the placing the ashes of the *parah adumah* on someone is beyond our understanding. King Solomon, known as the wisest of all men, even stated that he did not have an explanation for this commandment.

Sometimes, Hashem asks us to do things that we don't necessarily understand. In the same vein, when one is in recovery, he is also asked to do things which don't make sense. Many times, a recovering addict uses his intellect and guile to get him to where he is. He is able to rationalize his actions. He finds many reasons why he is not an addict and why he can do certain actions without hurting anyone—normalizing his addiction.

There is a smack in the face when one walks into the room of a 12-Step meeting and starts to take direction. There are meetings, affirmations, therapists, daily routines, and many other actions that might or might not make sense to an addict. It is imperative that if one is truly to find recovery, he has to be willing to take direction and do things that make no sense to him. How is saying something positive about myself every day stopping me from using? How can being of service and helping other people help me in my recovery? Going to ninety meetings in ninety days is a pain, and I don't see the value! On the contrary, one has to look at working his sobriety as he does at following Hashem's commandments. There is a reason, and it works if you work it, whether or not you understand the logic behind it. We don't need to understand everything because, in reality, we can't. I don't understand brain surgery, but I know it works. I don't have a clue as to how a four-million-pound object can blast into space, but I know it does. So, with recovery, one can see the countless number of women and men who enjoy sobriety through working their program. Just as with the laws that Hashem commanded us which we don't necessarily understand, so too, if we follow the "commandments" of the program, they will lead us towards a life of sobriety.

Balak

I remember when I was a child and I wanted to eat an entire bag of marshmallows. My mom said that it was not a good idea. I argued back and forth and made a convincing case for her to allow me to eat the entire bag of marshmallows. My mom knew what was going to happen, but she allowed me to learn for myself. A sore belly made me realize that it was not the best decision.

In *Parashas Balak*, we see a similar experience with the evil prophet Bilaam, where he basically says that he wants to go and work with the enemy of the Jewish people. It seems that Hashem kind of acquiesces and then Hashem gets mad at Bilaam, similar to the Jews when they spied out the land and then Hashem got angry. So, the rabbis ask: Do we have free will, or not?

In the Gemara, it clearly states that when it comes to certain things—such as your money, looks, height, and similar things—they are preordained. When it comes to whether you're a good person or not a good person, that's on you. That's not on Hashem. So, although everything is not in our hands, we do have free will.

When it comes to addiction, there is a similar argument. Some studies state that addiction is a predisposition, part of your DNA. The addict's brain structure is different and that causes him to act out with drugs, alcohol, or other addictions. It might be that if your parents were alcoholics or drug addicts that you might have a greater chance to be an addict. At the same time, just because you might be predisposed to certain qualities does not mean that you can't make choices so as to avoid certain outcomes. You can't give up and say that you don't need to work on it.

Pinchas

Have you ever gone to park your car and hit the car in front of or behind you? You quickly look around and see that nobody is watching. You question whether you should or shouldn't leave a note. You rationalize that everyone does it, that it's even been done to you, and that no one leaves a note. You are then filled with righteous indignation as you aren't doing anything differently from anyone else.

In *Parashas Pinchas*, Zimri, the slain Israelite from the previous parashah, whose crime was taking a Midianite woman and having relations with her in front of his brethren after being warned not to do so, is mentioned again along with stating that he was killed with the Midianite woman. The Gemara (*Sanhedrin* 82a) states that Zimri asked the question that if Moshe was married to a Midianite, why could he not also take a Midianite woman? This leaves out the fact that there was idolatry and inappropriate behavior going on at this time. Zimri convinced himself that since Moshe did something, he too could do the same thing. He did not understand the complexity of the situation. He also perverted Moshe's intent and twisted it to his own liking. He didn't realize that not everyone is the same. Many times, this type of thought process is what impacts addicts. They see what someone else is doing and they use the actions of that other person to justify their own, or they see what other people are doing and feel that they are entitled to do the same.

For example, there is nothing wrong with having wine for *Kiddush*, it's part of the mitzvah—unless, of course, you are an alcoholic. Or, they might see someone have a piece of cake and they justify that they, too, should have a piece of cake. The only problem is that they struggle with eating issues and, as a result, they won't have just one piece of cake.

The list goes on and on. The addict needs to realize that he is not the same. What one person can do, the addict can't necessarily do. Also, an addict tries to fit his situation into some else's situation. Zimri failed to understand that Moshe was not Zimri, and Zimri was not Moshe. He allowed this notion of being the same to overtake him, whereby he made a decision that cost him his life. Unfortunately, many addicts make these same types of decisions. They see what other people are doing and want to think that they are the same. But, just as a diabetic can't eat whatever he wants and someone on heart medication should not bungee jump, a recovering addict must temper his desire to be the same. There are things that he can't do, and he needs to accept that. Instead of being consumed by what he can't do, an addict should focus on the blessings that he has in front of him. And, go ahead, make *Kiddush* on peach grape juice; it's mighty tasty.

Matos

I remember playing with my Atari video game as a child and loving every minute of it. Except, when I didn't. As the famous line from William Congreve's play, *The Mourning Bride*, goes, "Hell has no fury like a child who just lost a video game..." Okay, maybe that is not the exact quote, but the anger that ensued after a lost game might entail throwing the joysticks, kicking the wall, and breaking something minor. All of these expressions of anger can be attributed to not only children but to adults alike. When something doesn't go our way or we are wronged in some sort of way, our reaction might be deemed inappropriate. How many people know someone who has broken a television because the sports game didn't go how he wanted it to or made some other poor decision in his rage. As the Talmud states in *Pesachim* 113b, "The life of those who can't control their anger is not a life." In *Hilchos Deos* 2:3, the *Rambam* said that when someone becomes angry it is as if he has become an idolater. These are some pretty strong condemnations of anger.

In *Parashas Matos*, it states, "Moshe became angry with the officers of the army..." and later Elazar, the Kohen Gadol, had to answer a question because Moshe did not know the answer. According to *Rashi*, because Moshe was angry a few verses earlier, the answer was concealed from him. This was at least the third time that the Torah notes Moshe's anger and that there was some sort of consequence. Anger can suffocate us.

For those in recovery, anger can be an obstacle, just like it was with Moshe, except with even greater consequences. As it states in the tenth step of the Big Book of Alcoholics Anonymous, we can suffer a hangover from negative emotions, including anger. These stay with us and impact the recovery process. Sometimes an addict will give himself permission to be angry—what's known as righteous indignation. This is when we feel we are right, we are on a moral and spiritual high ground, and we don't care about those who don't see things our way. This moral high ground rarely results in a positive outcome. An addict cannot allow himself to hold on to anger and allow it to run his life. Ultimately, the anger turns into resentment, which turns into a "dry drunk," one who does not use a substance but does not have balance or sobriety in any other aspect of their life, which then will lead to a loss of sobriety. As Step 10 notes, taking personal inventory allows someone to constantly look at his part in any situation and clean up the mess. If I am upset about something, what is it really about? The anger that fuels someone will ultimately bring harm to him. If Moshe, the greatest prophet in all of Israel, known as one of the greatest prophets the world has ever seen, suffered due to his anger, how much more so should we work to eliminate anger from our lives.

Mas'ei

"The assembly shall rescue the killer from the hand of the avenger of the blood, and the assembly shall return him to his city of refuge" (*Bamidbar* 35:25). The verse tells us about someone who kills someone as a result of carelessness or by complete accident. He did not plan to kill someone, but due to his behavior there was a fatal accident. The Torah tells us that this person is not killed, but instead moved to one of the forty-eight cities where the family of the person who he killed could not hurt him. The killer was required to stay in this city as a way to atone for his mishap. This move benefits everyone involved.

Something so traumatic can reverberate and there might be unintended consequences. So too, is it with someone on his road to recovery. Many people make a physical change, which follows the dictum, when you change your place, you change your *mazal* (luck). Whereas an unintentional killer must change his physical location, the person in recovery must change his mental and spiritual location. He must go somewhere else because his "location" is not working. It is a place where heartache, pain, and torment exist. Shame fills his mental and emotional state. Whereas this new place might be strange and difficult, it is a place of recovery.

While the unintentional killer needs to wait for the Kohen Gadol to die before he can leave and go back home, someone in recovery needs that "aha moment," the moment where they finally get it, before they can go back to their old physical location. Whether it is a physical location which might be harmful to him, or a place in his thoughts which will cause him to relapse, his patience is needed until he can step back into that location. Too many recovering addicts fool themselves into thinking that they can go back to their old location before they're ready.

This can have unfortunate consequences, which I have seen too many times, including even death. If the unintentional killer goes back to his city of origin, there is a real chance he will die; so too is it with the recovering addict. The patience, contemplation, and work are needed before he can take that journey back to where he was before he was addicted.

Devarim

S igns are around us all the time. We look up and see billboards that entice us to purchase certain items. A tall palm tree might inform us that we are in California, while tree ferns might let us know that we are in Australia. There are many signs that guide us to where we need to be. *Sefer Devarim* is called the *Mishneh Torah* because it is a repetition of prior events. It details everything that the Jewish people needed to remember before they entered the Eretz Yisrael. *Parashas Devarim* starts with Moshe speaking to the Jewish people, mentioning a series of places, a few of which don't actually exist. The rabbis teach us that these places, such as Dai-zahav, Paran, and Tophel, to name a few, were codes for derogatory actions that the Jews did during their time in the desert. For example, "Dai-zahav" means "enough gold." This was in reference to the golden calf that was created and worshiped. These signs, albeit negative ones, were to be reminders to the Jewish people to trudge along gleefully as they entered Yisrael, while reminding them how some of their trials and tribulations were caused by their own actions. Even though Moshe was not explicit, he was able to send a message.

As people in recovery know, there are many signs that can remind someone of his past behaviors and actions. A smell, a taste, a specific street, or even a person might cause some sort of euphoric recall and memory of past behaviors. These signs can be helpful indicators to remind oneself to stay away from these actions. As with the Jewish people, the signs don't have to be explicit, shameful, and embarrassing, but can be gentle reminders of what can happen when one is not working his program. A person does not need to tell everyone that he used to celebrate with cocaine every time that he won a court case, but instead, he can remember that those were the actions of his past and that he is creating new pathways to the future. If there was a certain street that you used to cruise to pick up people or places that involved scoring drugs, these are places best avoided until you have achieved sobriety.

Once you have achieved sobriety, if you are unable to avoid these places, the memory can be one of nudging you to work your program and incentivize you to stay sober. It is not an easy task. As we see, it took B'nei Yisrael forty years to enter Eretz Yisrael. It will also take time and patience as one works his program. But, by using these signs, they can help guide you to a new path and new signs that can be part of a road to recovery.

Va'eschanan

As a kid, I can't remember how many times my parents told me the exact same thing multiple times. If you are married or are in a committed relationship, you might experience this phenomenon of having your partner tell you the same thing many times. It's like Groundhog Day, where you question why you need to hear the same thing that you have been told before. You get it and don't need to hear it again.

The Jewish people could have felt the same way as Moshe was about to pass away, and he repeated the Ten Commandments, the same commandments that were told to them in *Parashas Yisro*. The Ten Commandments were originally given amidst open miracles, such as the hearing and visually impaired being able to hear and see, and people's souls left their bodies because the voice of Hashem was too great for them. So, we fast forward to this week's Torah portion and instead of Hashem, Moshe repeats the Ten Commandments. There are some differences between the two versions. Most specifically, the fourth, fifth, and tenth commandments have changes. Otherwise, they are almost an exact repetition of the Ten Commandments as they appear in *Parashas Yisro*. The commentators give many reasons for the two sets of the Ten Commandments. One understanding is that this was thirty-nine years later so people needed a review of the basic concepts, especially since there were new people to hear them.

I look at these two sets of the Ten Commandments as being akin to the 12 Steps. When someone is new in recovery, the first time he hears the 12 Steps, his world is rocked. There might be a strong reaction, a feeling of euphoria, or a feeling of being overwhelmed. There might be a visceral reaction or a call to action. Regardless of one's reaction to hearing the 12 Steps, his world is forever changed. When B'nei Yisrael heard the Ten Commandments for the first time, their world was forever changed. The repetition of the Ten Commandments by Moshe should have impacted everyone because, in the thirty-nine years that had passed, hopefully, everyone who was hearing them for the second time had changed.

We are not stagnant creatures. We should be forever growing and moving forward. When we constantly work the 12 Steps, there should be different and new understandings for the same steps previously traversed because we regularly find ourselves in different places in our lives. We are not the same as we used to be, and we see and experience things differently as time marches forward. Sobriety, like life, is not stagnant. It is something that must constantly be worked on, and it changes based on where you are in your life. May we continue to grow and utilize the 12 Steps as we move to serenity and long-term sobriety.

Eikev

When I was a child, the tragedy of the space shuttle Challenger took place, when it exploded during take-off. I remember that there was a teacher on board, and I remember feeling very sad. It was a snowy day, so we weren't at school, which, to me, was a miracle. For my parents, the idea that there was even a space shuttle at all was a miracle.

In *Parashas Eikev*, Moshe describes the miracles that Hashem did for the Jewish people when they left Egypt, as a way for B'nei Yisrael to not be fearful as they entered Eretz Yisrael. He then says Hashem will send a "*tzirah*" to protect the Jewish people. *Rashi* explains that a *tzirah* is a flying insect that shoots out bile which causes impotence and blindness. As I think of this and the many incredible miracles that Hashem did in the Torah, I hear the voices of doubt.

The *tzirah* is akin to the miracles that occur for people in recovery. As people go through the steps and work their program, they are witnesses to open miracles. People who could never hold down a job, or be in a committed relationship, or stay sober, suddenly experience such things. The impossible becomes possible. These open miracles have millions of people who have witnessed them. For every person that, unfortunately, loses his life, there are those who have been saved. These miracles defy logic and intellect. Yet, they are no less miraculous, no less amazing, but that much more believable.

The recovering addict needs to do exactly what the Torah states in regard to the *tzirah*. The *tzirah* was sent when the people were doing what they were supposed to be doing. It didn't happen in a vacuum, but with work and following a directive. So too, the miracles in the program can only occur when you are doing the work; they don't just happen. When you choose recovery and follow the program, setting your sights on sobriety, you will see open miracles. Things that you never expected to happen will happen. Life will also happen and there will be challenges, but there will also be miracles.

Re'eh

I remember when I was a kid and I got a pack of baseball cards. Within those cards was that precious piece of gum. All my friends wanted some, and it was so difficult to part with any of that precious gum. It was stale and tasteless, but so special because it came with the cards.

In *Parashas Re'eh*, there is a commandment that states, *"asser t'asser"* or you shall certainly tithe. This verse is understood by our Sages as a call for action. One's initial thought of giving is that he is taking from what he has and giving it to someone else. Our tradition teaches us that what is ours is actually a gift from Hashem and it is meant to be shared. There is an innate fear that one is going to miss out or lose something if he shares it with someone else. The Talmud in *Taanis* 9a clearly states that the opposite will happen when one gives: he will actually enrich himself as opposed to losing out.

This contrary action is what we tell people in recovery on a regular basis. Logic dictates that when I am an addict, what do I have to offer anyone? The opposite is true. The twelfth step of Alcoholics Anonymous teaches recovering addicts to carry the message of recovery to other people. Hashem imbued each person with gifts that make him uniquely qualified to give to others. Believe it or not, one of these gifts can be that you suffered and struggled with your addiction. There are numerous parts of ourselves that we can tithe. Hashem has blessed each person with the ability to give, which not only empowers the receiver, but also the one doing the giving. We should look inward to find these gifts and tithe.

Shoftim

I still remember as he walked into class, fifteen minutes late. The teacher, himself a former athlete, smiled and looked almost with reverence as this young man walked into class. Everyone else in the class looked around but understood exactly what was going on. He was a star athlete and, of course, he got treated differently and wasn't subjected to the same requirements as everyone else. This was the antithesis of what people felt should happen, but we understood that it was what it was.

In *Parashas Shoftim*, the mitzvah for a king of Israel to carry a *Sefer Torah* with him at all times is discussed. The rabbis understand that the reason that the king needs to carry a *Sefer Torah* was so that he would always remember that Hashem is with him and act accordingly. Because the king had almost unfettered power, including the ability to execute someone, his ego needed to be kept in check. Another reason, as explained by the rabbis, is that the king needed to remember that he was chosen for this job, and it was due to this that he was made king, not because of some inherent greatness that he naturally possessed. He was no better than anyone else.

As people in recovery know, they often have extreme of feelings about themselves that colors how they feel. There is either the "I am the most unworthy person, and if anyone really knew who I was, he would not like me," or the "I deserve this and that and if I hadn't been wronged I wouldn't be in this position." This is called the "terminally unique syndrome." The ego or lack of ego creates almost a bifurcated understanding of oneself. The mitzvah of the king can teach recovering addicts that Hashem is always with us. The mitzvah to carry a *Sefer Torah* should remind them that we are who we are for a reason. We are not better than anyone else and, at the same time, we are not worthless either. Instead, this symbol of carrying Hashem's law is to remind us of our inherent worth and, in turn, of the worth of everyone else. If we can keep this balance, it will allow us to see that the task that we have is staying on course. Just as the king had his course and a reminder to stay on it, following the 12 Steps will help keep a balanced and realistic approach to how we see ourselves and the world. So, remember we are never as bad as we think we are, and we also are not the best human beings ever created. We, like everyone else, are a work in progress. So, keep Hashem with you and you will be able to "trudge the road of happy destiny."

Ki Setzei

Have you ever been excited to go somewhere? As a kid, I couldn't wait to go to the beach. My family was getting ready to pack up the car, and I was making sure that I had everything for the trip. Sunscreen. Check. Water. Check. Hat. Check. Towel. Check. Fashionable sunglasses, of course! Then my parents said to grab the umbrella from the garage. Besides looking like a dork at the beach, I was ready to go. You have a hat and sunscreen, why do you need more shade? The entire purpose of the beach is to lie out in the sun all day. My parents wanted to make sure that there wouldn't be too much sun exposure. They were being cautious, maybe a little extra cautious because they understood that my grandfather passed away from skin cancer, but they didn't want to burden me with this information.

In this parashah, we have the innocuous mitzvah of making sure that we have guardrails for our roof when we build a new house. Of all the things that we need to make sure a house has, putting guardrails on your roof might not be the first thing that comes to mind. Yet, the next verse states that by building guardrails we will make sure that someone does not fall and die on our property. The *Sefer Hachinuch* teaches us that when we build guardrails in any area that is in our possession, like a pit or a ditch, "We remove the obstacles and sources of harm from all our habitations." So, we go above and beyond to make sure that we do not have someone injured or die on our property.

In recovery, addicts constantly must build guardrails around all aspects of their life. These guardrails ensure that there are steps that are taken before the addict can relapse. For example, many recovering alcoholics won't go to a bar, won't have alcohol in their home, and won't attend parties where they know there might be a lot of drinking. They take these steps in order to ensure that they won't be tempted to drink. People in Overeaters Anonymous will make sure that if they are a guest in someone's house, they let them know which foods that they can and can't eat, so that they don't come for a meal and wind up not having anything to eat. Someone who struggles with looking at inappropriate materials might only purchase a phone with very limited features which makes it impossible to look up inappropriate things on his phone. These precautions might seem trivial to those not in recovery, but the guardrails that these recovering addicts put up are essential to their sobriety. Just as the guardrails the Torah describes are meant to save lives, so too a recovering addict puts up guardrails to save a life—his own—and, in turn, the lives of his family.

Ki Savo

We all had someone growing up whom we looked up to. It might have been a sibling, parent, friend, rabbi, or a coach. Everything we did, we wanted to emulate this person. Maybe, as we got older, we started to see some chinks in that person's armor, and we realized that he was human and made mistakes like everyone else. *Parashas Ki Savo* contains the commandment to emulate the good attributes of Hashem. That is a pretty heavy task, but, as we know, we are not asked to do things that we are not able to do.

What does it mean to emulate Hashem? The *Rambam* states that when we act compassionately towards someone, we should do so in a way that Hashem would do. Being compassionate is very connected to Step 9 of the 12 Steps of Alcoholics Anonymous. Step 9 states: "Make direct amends to such people wherever possible, except when to do so would injure them or others." We have made mistakes, so we make a list of those mistakes and then reach out to apologize. This is similar to what we do every year before the High Holidays. Yet, to emulate Hashem's way means the compassion needs to be whole and complete.

This brings up the question, what about compassion for oneself? Many times, the way we see the world, we can look at our mistakes and recognize those whom we have harmed. We might even be able to make amends. Yet, there is something missing. We ask for forgiveness, but we never forgive ourselves. In recovery, many addicts are very judgmental of themselves. They are constantly aware of the pain and suffering that they have inflicted on other people. They beat themselves up and do not allow themselves to heal.

There is a famous saying in the recovery world, "I'm judging my insides by somebody else's outside." How many times have we seen people who look like they have it all—everything appears perfect. They have happy pictures of a beautiful house, car, family, and lifestyle, but, in reality, their world is crumbling apart. We desire what we think they have, what we don't have, and we judge ourselves on this. So how does all of this relate to emulating Hashem and compassion? The notion of emulating Hashem means that we also must have compassion and empathy for ourselves. This does not mean that we don't work on ourselves or take inventory of our actions. Instead, we need to understand that life is a process. We're not there yet. We're each a work in progress. Once we stop having compassion and empathy for ourselves, we tend to stop working on ourselves.

Nitzavim

I remember as a child when I broke my mom's vase, and I tried to glue it back together. It was an assortment of mismatched pieces. The vase looked terrible, but I was hoping my mom wouldn't notice. Of course, she did. As I had to apologize with my shoulders slumped, I knew that I might get in trouble. The most difficult part was actually saying what I did was wrong and that I would not do it again.

In *Parashas Nitzavim*, we are told that the Jewish people will eventually repent for all the deeds that they did that were not good. "You will return unto Hashem, your G-d, and listen to his voice" (*Devarim* 30:2). *Teshuvah* (repentance) is a key component to our relationship with Hashem and other people. The *Rambam* goes into great detail in the *Mishneh Torah* about doing *teshuvah*. One point that he elaborates upon is the idea of verbally expressing our sins, called *viduy*. The idea of verbally recalling one's sins allows one to not just internally know what he did wrong, but actually make a point of saying it out loud to Hashem.

In recovery, one of the keys is to make amends to everyone whom we wronged. These steps, 8 and 9, ask one to make a list of everyone whom he wronged and then expressly make amends except when to do so would harm him or others. Making amends to someone, face-to-face, is about expressly allowing the words to come off of your lips and say, "I'm sorry." Instead of just internalizing the sin, you put it out in the universe. Saying sorry is difficult, especially when you say it to someone's face. By allowing the other person to have the opportunity to see that you are taking ownership of your actions, it gives him the ability to actually forgive you. Instead of a half-hearted apology, you see that your actions actually have consequences. This also allows the healing process to begin—for you and the person whom you've hurt.

Vayeilech

Do you remember your first concert? There were lots of people gathered together for a single cause, to hear their favorite artist. Everyone was waiting with enthusiasm, looking forward to hearing his favorite songs being played. Each word that came out of the singer's mouth, you followed along, and you knew every chord and every tune. But you were not the only one. There were throngs of people who were in the same situation. They all sang with you, mesmerized by the transcendence of hearing your favorite song in person, with thousands of your closest friends! The power of the crowd was amazing. The energy and enthusiasm were felt by everyone. The lead singer knew exactly what to do to make sure everyone was in sync and was able to connect to his message.

The second to the last mitzvah (commandment) in the Torah is "*hakhel*." This was the mitzvah to hold a public Torah reading. This mitzvah occurs once every seven years during Sukkos. The entire nation would gather to hear part of the Torah being read by the king. As the previous Lubavitcher Rebbe noted, this mitzvah strengthened and aroused the inner faith of those who attended. This strength could carry one as he moved forward in his day-to-day life.

There are some 12-Step meetings that can carry those who participate in them. There might not be crowds of more than thirty people, but they are just as substantial. When there is a speaker meeting, which is one that features someone who has reached sobriety, sometimes for a substantial amount of time, and that person shares his story, the participants then use what the speaker shares with them to guide them. The opportunity to listen to a speaker who has been to the depths of the abyss and come back to talk about it can be very powerful. The energy in the room can be palpable, as the participants hang on to every word that the speaker shares. You listen not only because it is moving, but to learn how it can be done. The speaker is sharing with you a playbook to master sobriety. Regardless of how much sobriety the speaker has achieved, the poignancy of what he shares can help each person in the room with his own road to recovery.

Haazinu

I remember when my parents told me and my siblings to do something and it would go in one ear and out the other. Why? We knew it was just another chore. Perhaps, it was the famous talk about thinking first. Whatever it might be, my siblings knew the deal. You knew that if it was really important, your parents would tell you again.

As Moshe was about to ascend to Har Navo for his eventual death, he tells B'nei Yisrael, "Observe all the words of this Torah. For it is not an empty thing for you. Rather, it is your life." *Rashi* understands this verse, "For it is not an empty thing for you" as meaning that, when one follows the Torah, he is rewarded immensely. He interprets this reward as referring to one's life, and hence, the next verse. So, following the Torah is a reward in and of itself because it gives a person life.

The same can be said for recovering addicts. Working the 12 Steps are an important lifeline. Each part of the process builds on the other parts of the process. It is not an empty thing, but it is your life. As anyone who is in recovery or has a friend or family member in recovery knows, it really is a life-or-death proposition. There are too many people who have lost their lives to addiction. According to recent statistics, in 2017, five percent of all deaths worldwide were from alcohol and almost 600,000 deaths worldwide were from drug overdose. These statistics do not take into account all the other addictions that impoverished families, broke up households, and caused mental and physical anguish. The 12 Steps are not the only way to conquer addiction, but working the steps breathes new life into the addict. The addict sees that recovery is an option and that there are alternatives to addiction. He sees the multilayered aspects of his addiction. Recovery and the 12 Steps are not an empty thing; rather, it is your life. Literally.

V'zos Haberachah

It's so hard to let go. We sometimes hold onto grudges and pain. Holding on does not help anyone but makes things more difficult. According to research conducted by psychologist John Cacioppo, people focus on the negative more than the positive. They make decisions, pay more attention, and learn more from negative experiences than positive ones. They don't let go of these negative experiences so easily.

In the final parashah of the Torah, Moshe passes away. The way that the Torah describes the death of Moshe is beautiful. "And Moshe, the servant of Hashem, died there, in the Land of Moav, by the mouth of Hashem" (*Devarim* 34:5). *Rashi* notes that "the mouth of Hashem" means a kiss by Hashem. According to the Talmud in *Mo'ed Katan* 28a, this means a death directly from Hashem as opposed to an intermediary. And another Talmudic reference from *Berachos* 8a notes that this is the most ideal way to die, since the soul leaves the body without any resistance, like a hair being pulled from a glass of milk. The soul is unattached to this world, ready to move forward in the spiritual realm. The Talmud also describes the opposite situation, where the soul leaves the body with resistance, compared to wool being pulled from thistles, where every move is delicate and painful.

When a person enters recovery, it is common for him to bring a lot of baggage and pain with him. Every slight and difficult experience is pulling at the addict. All the pain and emotional baggage continues to hold the recovering addict in his current position. Only when he is able to let go and release the past is he able to move forward. The ultimate goal for the recovering addict is to forgive, ask for forgiveness, and to move forward without expectations or holding onto the past. As a famous adage notes, expectations are resentments waiting to happen. Once he starts to let go of his hurt, pain, and resentments and move forward in recovery, the recovering addict can move forward. They will notice that just as the hair which can be pulled out of the milk with relative ease, they are able to navigate life on life's terms and not live where every move is like wool stuck in thistle, where every move is filled with pain, concern, and continual difficulty. It is this sort of recovery that one yearns for just as Moshe moved forward, hand in hand with Hashem so to speak, the recovering addict moves forward with Hashem.

Holidays

Rosh Hashanah

A Different Form of Tzedakah

Rosh Hashanah is the start of the new year. It is a time to start again, reset our clocks, and take a look at the last year. We see what we did right and wrong and look to move forward. There are so many things that we do to get ourselves in the spirit. As with any new year, we make resolutions on how this year will be different and how we will get it right. One of the tools that we have to help guide us is the principle found in the holy prayer "*Unesaneh Tokef,*" written by Rabbi Amnon, *z"l,* of Mainz, Germany. The prayer mentions three principles: *teshuvah* (repentance), *tefillah* (prayer), and tzedakah (charity). The idea of repentance allows us to look at what we have done and how we can do it better. Prayer includes having greater intention and being more focused on the words that we say. With regard to charity, we give of our time and resources. These three things are ways that enable us to change whatever judgment that we might have received for the upcoming year.

Working with recovering addicts, tzedakah is seen as one of the biggest indicators to help in recovery. When we think of tzedakah, many of us think of just giving money. According to the Talmud (*Gittin* 7a and *Ketubot* 67b) tzedakah is so much more than that. Tzedakah is not only with our physical resources, but also our personal, emotional, and spiritual resources. This includes giving of our time and ourselves. There is no place where this is seen so selflessly than by those who work the 12 Steps of Recovery. As Rabbi Dr. Twerski, *z"l,* noted, where else would one find someone calling at 2:00 in the morning for support and receiving it? Step 12 of any 12-Step program is, "Having had a spiritual awakening as the result of these steps, we tried to carry this message to alcoholics, and to practice these principles in all our affairs." This means that one can walk into any 12-Step meeting and almost always find someone whom he has never met, but who is ready to lend a helping hand. And it is not unusual for an addict to have more than one person be there to help him. Unlike the idea of giving with the intent of receiving or having some sort of benefit, this is not the case. You have a famous musician giving out his number to an out of work electrician, or an Orthodox rabbi helping an African American Muslim teacher, or a waiter helping a CEO of a Fortune Five Hundred Company. And yet, none of it matters. It is the idea of giving back and being selfless.

This type of tzedakah is not something one can write with a checkbook but comes from within. We share a common mission, to elevate the world and bring spirituality to the mundane. When we are not blinded by what award we might receive for our generosity, but instead, motivated by how we can save and impact one life at a time, it is the true essence of tzedakah according to the *Rambam's* eight different levels of giving. This type of selflessness does not need to be for only those in a 12-Step program but can be brought down to anyone at any time. As we move towards the New Year and think about Rabbi Amnon's three principles that can help shape the destiny of the upcoming year, let's try to emulate the twelfth step when we are giving back. Being open, wholesome, true, and willing to go that extra mile, even when it is not convenient for us.

Yom Kippur
Teshuvah and Addiction Recovery

As someone who works intimately with those in addiction recovery, I am always looking to see the integration of the 12 Steps of Alcoholics Anonymous (AA or any 12-Step program) and the Torah. I am grateful that Rabbi Dr. Twerski started this concept many years ago and has shared a lot of work on this subject.

As we are in the midst of the Aseres Yemei Teshuvah, we are preparing to gain total forgiveness on Yom Kippur. As we know, Yom Kippur can wipe away the transgressions between us and Hakadosh Baruch Hu. But what about all our transgressions *bein adam l' chaveiro* (between man and his fellow man) and the hurt that we have caused the people in our life? As the *Rambam* states in the *Mishneh Torah* 2:9, "*Teshuvah* and Yom Kippur only atone for sins between man and Hashem...However, sins between man and man—for example, someone who injures a colleague, curses a colleague, steals from him, or the like—will never be forgiven until he gives his colleague what he owes him and appeases him." We also know that we can always seek forgiveness, but that the Aseres Yemei Teshuvah is the best time as it states in *Yeshayahu* 55:6, "Seek Hashem when He is to be found."

These two aspects of seeking *teshuvah*, directly asking one for forgiveness and asking at the most opportune time, are integrated into the 12 Steps of AA. Step 9 states, "Made direct amends to such people whenever possible, except when to do so would injure them or others." Making this direct apology after completing the first 8 Steps is imperative in the recovery process of the addict. Coming face-to-face, making amends, making restitution when possible, and then taking the course of action to not repeat the same wrongdoing, brings the recovering addict towards recovery. Just like one does not receive complete atonement on Yom Kippur until he asks for forgiveness directly from the individuals whom he has hurt, so too one does not truly complete the 12 Steps until he has made direct amends.

Regarding the idea of asking for forgiveness during this auspicious time when Hashem is close, one who is recovering from addiction should not immediately ask for forgiveness from everyone. Rather he should wait until he is ready, and the time is right. There are so many issues that a person needs to work on, including connecting to his Higher Power (Hashem) and admitting powerlessness to his addiction among other things. This gives him the ability to ask for forgiveness in a more authentic way.

As we work towards doing a complete *teshuvah* in preparation for Yom Kippur, we can think about a recovering addict who tirelessly tries to make amends for his complete recovery—understanding that seeking forgiveness from those whom we have hurt is the only way that both recovery and *teshuvah* can take place. May we all merit to have a complete *teshuvah* this year.

Sukkos

S ukkos is a festive holiday. We have gone through the trials and tribulations of the high holidays, and now it is time for enjoyment. Yet, we are commanded to go out into a sukkah, or temporary hut, for seven days. "You shall dwell in a sukkah for a seven-day period." There are many explanations regarding dwelling in a sukkah for seven days. One understanding is that we are reminded of the fragility of life and that, ultimately, Hashem is our protector; our buildings and structures are not what protect us. The belief that there is a Hashem who loves us, guides us, protects us, and wants what is best for us can help us through challenging episodes in life. So too, is it with sobriety. We can build up structures to keep us sober and protect us, but ultimately, it is the internal work that we do that is the most significant. One of those steps is Step 2 of the 12 Steps, "We came to believe a power greater than ourselves could restore us to sanity." Once we realize that our power is defined by our perception of things and our need for absolute control is not reality, we can turn our life over to a greater power. This power is Hashem. We go out into the sukkah during a time where it might not be the most convenient or where one might not think the timing is the best. In many parts of the world, the fall season includes rain, colder weather, and wind. If we went into the sukkah when it might be natural to go, then we would be going in spring or summer. That would make the most sense, especially since we initially dwelled in sukkos after leaving Egypt in the springtime. One of the reasons that we do this is to show our absolute belief and trust in Hashem while demonstrating our willingness to believe that Hashem has our best interest at heart. This same idea can be applied to our daily lives and the chaos that can ensue from addiction. We are in a storm, so to speak, and everything around us does not make sense. Yet, those who are willing go outside their normal boundaries and dwell in the sukkah of Hashem. This temporary structure, which seems flimsy, offers physical and spiritual protection.

So too, one who allows himself to fully believe that there is a power greater than himself can be restored to sanity, because while using, everything around the addict is anything but sane. No amount of control could stop the addiction and only once he allows his Higher Power to take control is he able to step into that protection, which, similar to a sukkah, looks flimsy, but in reality, is so much more than it seems.

Simchas Torah

We experience absolute joy when we participate in Simchas Torah services. There is the singing, dancing, amazing *hakafos*, finishing the Torah, and starting it anew. It's all filled with a lot of pomp and circumstance, as kids fill up on candy and treats. The *hakafos* refer to the dancing with the Torah around the bimah that we do on Simchas Torah. There are numerous reasons offered for why we do this. The circuits around the bimah are described by the *Rama*, who codified the Ashkenazi Jewish law, by stating, "All these customs are ways through which we rejoice with and show honor for the Torah." The finishing of the Torah and circling the bimah are given a deeper meaning by the *Rambam*, who explains that these circles demonstrate that we should avoid extremes in life, just like a circle is similar in all aspects so we need to find that balance in life.

The idea of a circle bringing balance is one way those who work certain 12-Step programs find balance with their addiction. There is an activity called the three circles. It is an activity that one can use whether he is struggling with addiction or just working on improving a certain character trait in his life. One draws three circles, an inner, middle, and outer circle. The outer circle represents activities that help one grow as a human being. These are things that you enjoy doing, build self-esteem, and add to spiritual, mental, emotional, and physical growth. For some people, this might be a walk, a swim, prayer, reading a book, or spending time with certain people. Think of it as a green light; you keep these activities going as they build you up. The middle circle represents things that you prefer to avoid and cautions you that you might need to check your behavior. For example, you may notice that when you eat a certain food that you get grumpy, or if you discuss politics that you start to get angry, or when you don't get enough sleep, you might not be yourself. Think of it like a yellow traffic light, a warning sign that you need to slow down. The inner circle represents activities that you want to avoid, as these are harmful for your well-being. For an addict who is recovering from overeating this might include cake, ice cream, or other foods which send the person in a downward spiral. The idea of the circles is that they are not the same for any one person. One person struggles with anger issues, another with internet addictions, and another with a lack of patience, and they all will work their circles very differently. It is a way to evaluate and keep tabs on your activities and continue to grow spiritually and make progress towards recovery.

Going back to the *hakafos* for Simchas Torah, the circle embodies this notion of avoiding extremes. Keeping that balance and middle of the road approach can help us learn to live a life of meaning and steadiness, one where we are proud of the person who we are and the one who we are becoming.

Chanukah

Chanukah is a miraculous holiday, during which we love spending time with our family, eating lots of fried food, and remembering how we overcame assimilation and rededicated the Beis Hamikdash. There are numerous stories of heroism from then, but one of the most famous stories is about our heroine Yehudis, which seems to be compiled from a few different stories. The Syrian-Greeks would defile Jewish brides before they were married. Many Jews either had weddings underground or just did not get married to avoid the vicious decree. According to one version of the story, Yehudit met with the King, had a feast with him, got him drunk, and cut off his head. The Jews felt liberated by these actions. These heinous enactments, whenever they were instituted throughout our history, were placed to destroy the *kedushah* of Jewish marriage and to denigrate our holy women.

Today, as we celebrate Chanukah, we may not be fighting the Syrian-Greeks and their disturbing enactments, but we still have a vile perpetrator that is bent on destroying and defiling the sanctity of our marriages: pornography. According to recent studies published by Covenant Eyes (though Hub and others), thirty-five percent of all downloads from the internet are inappropriate materials. Forty million Americans regularly visit inappropriate sites and seventy percent of men aged eighteen to twenty-four visit these sites at least once a month.

This has even impacted those who are a part of the Torah-observant community. Many men are trying to find a *shidduch*, but they have these inappropriate images imprinted on their brains, resulting in unrealistic views of what marriage and intimacy should look like. Those who are already married also either bring this into their marriage or venture out and start looking at the inappropriate images available to them. During the pandemic, the numbers became even more startling, with an increase of anywhere between ten to fifty percent in people looking up inappropriate materials. Just as our Yehudit cut off the head of a military leader, so too, do we need to shed light and eradicate the scourge of inappropriate material that infects our homes. May we merit to sanctify our homes as the Beis Hamikdash was sanctified.

Tu B'Shevat

Deeper Insights

Tu B' Shevat is sometimes erroneously called the Jewish Arbor Day. Jews on the left cling to this notion and celebrate with great vigor, focusing on environmental concerns generally, including recycling and other well intended causes. Oftentimes, Jews on the right dismiss this notion and only see it as a day that we don't say *Tachanun*.

What can we learn to take into our everyday life from Tu B'Shevat? The Torah is replete with telling us to take care of our environment. Whether it is the Midrash from *Kohelet Rabbah* which states, "Look at my works! See how beautiful they are—how excellent! For your sake I created them all. See to it that you do not spoil and destroy My world; for, if you do, there will be no one else to repair it." Or the Mishnah in *Bava Basra* which tells us to set a distance for a tannery from the city due to the pungency of the process and how it will impact the inhabitants living closest to it.

The idea of taking care of the environment can also mean the environment in which we live, which includes the people who mean most to us, our family. Many times, we show one face on the outside, but, to those closest to us, we are not as meticulous in our actions or speech, showing an entirely different face when we're in private. This "environment," this higher standard to the outside world, needs to be maintained in private.

Another lesson we can learn is about *bal tashchis*, needless waste. Do you really need to use one more paper cup, another napkin, etc.? What about "needless waste" in our relationships? How much do we waste with being angry, resentful, and genuinely dissatisfied with those whom we love the most? They don't do what we want; they are not the person we want them to be; or they do things that upset us. We needlessly destroy precious time that could be used building these relationships and having them blossom like the trees that we plant. Just as agriculture takes time to blossom and requires lots of nutrients, nurturing, and patience, so do our relationships. If we don't put the appropriate time and internal resources into our relationships, they are bound to fail.

So, as we celebrate Tu B'Shevat this year and eat dried fruit from Eretz Yisrael, think about the environment, and don't say *Tachanun*, let us think about how we can use the lessons of the environment and needless waste to improve our own relationships and strengthen our connection to those closest to us.

Purim

A Hidden Message

Purim is a fun holiday. It is the day where we experience the excitement of dressing up as our favorite character, hearing the Megillah, shaking *graggers*, having a *seudas mitzvah*, and giving *mishloach manos* and *matanos l'evyonim*. As adults know, there is so much more to the history of Purim. The story is written in such a way that drinking plays a prominent role, whether in the text, through the lens of the rabbis, or through the laws associated with Purim. Be it Achashverosh's having a six-month party, the extra week of feasting and celebration that he made, or the obligation to drink until one can't distinguish between Haman and Mordechai, drinking plays a major role. As *Maseches Megillah* states, "One must drink on Purim until he cannot distinguish between cursing Haman and blessing Mordechai." Unfortunately, we have seen various communities where drinking has caused serious issues on Purim, including even death. As a former Hatzolah member, I've seen too many young people over-indulge with serious consequences on Purim. As a midrash from *Leviticus Rabbah* states about drinking, "The negative effect of wine is like a snakebite, separating life and death." We know the dangers of drinking on Purim and many synagogues take precautions so that young people are not influenced by excessive drinking and adults don't make decisions that have unintended consequences.

There is yet another serious and dark underbelly of Purim. That is the role of intimacy disorder. Since intimacy plays such an oversized role in our society, including in the media and the internet, one might tend to gloss over the continual innuendos in the story. One might ask how this is even in the equation regarding Purim. The definition of any addiction is the inability to stop something even when you know that it does not benefit you to continue, and the negative consequences are constantly ignored. This might include losing your dream job, your standing in the community, or, more importantly, your spouse, children, or even your life.

Let's set the scene, as Achashverosh was having his party for all his kingdom and then the extra week just for the people of Shushan, he asked his wife, Queen Vashti to come and show herself to his royal court. The Talmud understands that there were a couple of factors going on at this point. The first was that while the king was having his party, Queen Vashti was simultaneously having her own party. These were no ordinary parties. Besides the eating and drinking, the Talmud understands that the king and queen were participating in debauchery. One midrash from *Esther Rabbah* explains that the festivities were held in rooms where women would be comfortable doing inappropriate things that they might not normally be willing to do in front of other people. The rabbis of the Talmud went one step further and stated, "Both [Achashverosh and Vashti] had a sinful purpose [that is, they wanted to be intimate with the people at their party]." In other Talmudic literature, Vashti is described as someone who cheated frequently on her husband. The Midrash notes that her refusal to appear unclothed before her husband and his guests was because she was stricken with a skin disease, as otherwise she would have acquiesced without any issue. According to another understanding of the text, when Vashti was sentenced to die, the Midrash states that she sent a message to the King: "You were my father's steward, and you were accustomed to having unclothed harlots come before you. Now, that you have become king, you have not mended your ways." There is another description of Achashverosh as someone with an insatiable appetite for relations, so much so that the Talmud notes that his advisors, Bigsan and Teresh, wanted him dead because he requested to be intimate every night with Esther and this put an extra strain on them.

As stated by Dr. Michael Herkov, "Intimacy addiction is best described as a progressive intimacy disorder characterized by compulsive thoughts and acts. Like all addictions, its negative impact on the addict and on family members increases as the disorder progresses. Over time, the addict usually has to intensify the addictive behavior to achieve the same results." Achashverosh's compulsion led to the death of his wife and the death of two of his trusted advisors. It almost cost him his life, when his advisors tried to kill him. This would qualify as hitting bottom.

A national survey done in 2018 notes that between three and fifteen percent of the population struggle with some form of intimacy related issues. According to many studies, between five and eight percent of adults struggle with addiction to inappropriate material. Some of these numbers are cited by the Journal of the American Medical Association. The World Health Organization now recognizes looking at inappropriate materials as an addiction and a behavioral disorder. A famed explicit site recently stated that it received over 30 billion hits in 2018. According to Covenant Eyes, an Internet accountability software company, roughly 28,000 users are watching inappropriate materials every second. Users spend around $3,000 on this every second and over 40 million Americans visit inappropriate sites on a regular basis. Covenant Eyes also notes that fifty-six percent of divorce cases involved a partner's obsessive interest in inappropriate websites.

The lesson can guide us as we help our children and our families navigate their internet use, and realize that, maybe, there is a deeper message that the Megillah is trying to teach us during this time.

Pesach

Hitting Rock Bottom and Pesach

As we head into Pesach, there are many parts of the Seder to which we can connect. Whether it is the food, singing, retelling of the story, or the entertaining family customs, there is so much from which we can learn, including how to live life from the story of going from slavery to freedom, how to see Hashem in our everyday life, remembering that Hashem is the true G-d, and having gratitude—to name just a few. We can also learn about what recovering addicts know as hitting bottom. Hitting bottom is that place where a person's addiction has taken up so much of his life that there is no other option. There are two choices: getting clean or death.

Pharaoh experienced hitting bottom through the ten plagues. Much like someone in active addiction, each plague brought new hardships. Pharaoh felt the discomfort and was ready for a new life, until he wasn't. Many times, he seemed ready to relinquish power and turn over a new leaf, but his desire for control and absolute power took over. He knew best, yet he really didn't. His eyes told him one story, but his will told him something else. He experienced all kinds of hardships.

His willfulness led to suffering, the downfall of Egypt, the death of his family, and, according to many interpretations of the story, his own death in a painful and tormented manner. When one is active in his addiction, he often refuses to see the signs or plagues that impact his life. Much like the ten plagues, a person in active addiction sees the first plague as an aberration. Then, as the stakes start to rise, he makes excuses for each thing that he is encountering. Just as Pharaoh made excuses and got to the point where his heart was unable to be turned, so the addict puts up an impenetrable wall so that no amount of addiction or subsequent consequences will make a difference. Unfortunately, he might not change until the consequences get to such a point where even the death of his own child does not change his behavior. The midrash notes that before the plague of the *makkos bechoros* (death of the firstborn), there was a war between the Egyptians and the firstborns of Egypt, including Pharaoh's own son, who sought to send the Jews out so as to avoid the plague that would mean their deaths. Everyone else around him saw what was happening, but Pharaoh refused to see the signs. It was not until all was lost that he finally relinquished control and allowed the Jews to go out of Egypt. The consequences were dire, as they are for active addicts. Whether one is an addict, or just grapples with the day-to-day struggles which we all encounter, may we all have the ability to see the hand of Hashem in our lives and be open to support from those around us.

Tishah B'Av
Learning from Our Past

Tishah B'Av is the saddest day in the Jewish Calendar. The Mishnah teaches that there were five tragedies that occurred on this day, including the destruction of both Temples. Over the years, other events have taken place on this date as well, including the expulsion from Spain and the beginning of World War I. On Tishah B'Av, we remember all those who perished *al kiddush Hashem,* including those who were killed in the Holocaust.

There are so many things that we do to help elicit the sorrow that we are meant to experience on this day, including fasting, not bathing, and abstaining from meat and wine during the nine days prior. Yet, the *Artscroll Guide to Tishah B'Av* sums up the importance of the day with the following statement, "More than a day of lamenting, Tishah B'Av is a day of learning—learning essential lessons from the terrible errors of our past, so that we never repeat them again in the present or the future."

This sentence can, likewise, sum up the experience of those in recovery from substance abuse or other addictions. The last day that a person was not sober is akin to his personal Tishah B'Av. The remembrance of that day is called the person's "sobriety birthday." Unlike Tishah B'Av, the person receives a chip and is extolled for his sobriety, whether it be thirty days, six months, or however many years; it is a day of celebration. The celebration is that the person is doing the very thing that the above quote demonstrated, learning from his past and doing everything that he can not to repeat his mistakes in the future.

If the person in recovery is not learning from his past and learning essential lessons, he is doomed to repeat the same mistakes. The repetition of these lessons brings pain, hurt, suffering, struggles, hardships, desolation, and possibly even death. This is not different from the Jewish people. If we don't learn the lessons of prior events of Tishah B'Av then we are doomed to experience future events of Tishah B'Av. As Winston Churchill stated, "Those that fail to learn from history are doomed to repeat it."

An addict who is not in recovery repeats the same mistakes and the same issues. They may manifest in different areas, but they are the same issues. Just as the Jewish people have to learn from their past and draw a new course moving forward, so too does the addict. As the Sages taught (*Yerushalmi, Yoma* 1:1), any generation in which the Beis Hamikdash is not rebuilt, it is as if that generation destroyed it. For someone who is in active addiction, each day is Groundhog Day in which he plays out the same scenarios in a different way. Ultimately, he lacks sobriety, and he fights his inner demons while searching for a way to feel safe, secure, and loved. If he is able to learn from his past lessons, he will not continue to destroy his life, but instead, will grow and build himself up, one day at a time. This is a lesson that everyone can use, whether in recovery or not. Let's learn from our past, grow from it, and dedicate ourselves to a future that will include the coming of the Mashiach, *bimheirah b'yameinu.*

Conclusion

The Torah is the ultimate guidebook. No matter the time or place, it is a manual for how to live life. With that in mind, as I look at each and every parashah, I see some connection to what is going on right now in my life, in the world, and ultimately in regard to recovery. That is how my brain is wired. Looking at the wisdom of the Torah and finding ways to connect to contemporary issues has always been a way that Jews and non-Jews have connected the lessons of the Torah to the present. Seeing the G-dliness imbued within each person and the special spark that everyone has leads us to understand that being addicted is not an absolute definition of who a person is, but instead is a reflection of what they are experiencing in the moment.

As it is stated by the *mefarshim*, there is no problem for which G-d has not already created the remedy. Addiction is a scourge on our world. The World Health Organization (WHO) notes that there are 10 million deaths by alcohol, nicotine, and drugs a year and this does not include deaths by those suffering from food, gambling, sex, or other addictions. To put this in perspective, the current COVID pandemic has caused 5.5 million deaths since March 2020 worldwide. Addiction is an epidemic and by all estimates is increasing at a high rate and at an even higher rate since the COVID pandemic.

Learning from the Torah and the 12 Steps of Recovery are two ways to look at addictive actions and help lead a path to recovery. As with any issue, one is not alone. One needs G-d, family, friends, clergy, community, and sometimes even additional support. There is no shame in acknowledging that one has a struggle, and there is no blight on the family. There is no need for blaming and finger pointing but instead love, understanding, patience, and a well thought out plan for recovery.

May anyone who is dealing with addiction—whether themselves or with a friend or family member—find the source of strength that they need to help those struggling from addiction. My G-d bless you on your journey and know that you are loved.

Bibliography

Heinze, A. (September 1999). "The Americanization of Mussar: Abraham Twerski's Twelve Steps." *Judaism: A Quarterly Journal of Jewish Life and Thought.*

Sederer, L. (June 2015). "America Is Neglecting Its Addiction Problems." Retrieved March 10, 2016.

Steinberg, Paul. (Summer 2015). "Addiction in Body, Mind, and Jewish Spirituality." *Reform Journal,* pp. 17–35.

Sucarav, M. (November 2013). "Breaking Down the Shame." Retrieved March 25, 2016, from http://www.haaretz.com/blogs/the-fifth-question/1.557275).

Twelve Steps and Twelve Traditions. (1981). New York: Alcoholics Anonymous World Services.

Twerski, A. (2010). "Mussar and the 12 Steps." Retrieved March 4, 2016, from https://www.torahweb.org/torah/special/2010/dtwe_12steps.html

Twerski, A. J. (2000). *The Spiritual Self: Reflections on Recovery and God.* Center City, MN: Hazelden.

About the Author

Rabbi Dr. Chaim Tureff is from Tennessee. Rabbi Tureff's goal is to bring a connection between humanity and for everyone to relate to one another. He is the founder and director of STARS, which guides people struggling with addiction. It focuses on the spiritual component, and includes seminars, groups, and one-on-one coaching. He is also the *Rav Beit Sefer* at Pressman Academy in Los Angeles, a spiritual advisor at Soberman's Estate in Arizona, and a member of the Teachers on Fire *kollel* for *mechanchim*. He graduated from the UNC-Chapel Hill with honors and distinction in history, writing his honors thesis on the relationship between African Americans and Jewish Americans. He received his MA in elementary education from Columbia University and his Ed.D in Jewish Education from Gratz College with high honors, focusing on the role Judaism and spirituality play in helping recovering addicts. He received his *semichah* from Rav Dan Channen, *shlita*, and is an alumnus of the Darche Noam Yeshiva of Jerusalem and Rabbinical College of America in Morristown, New Jersey.

Rabbi Tureff is married and blessed to have a family. Please feel free to contact him at Rav.Meir18@gmail.com.

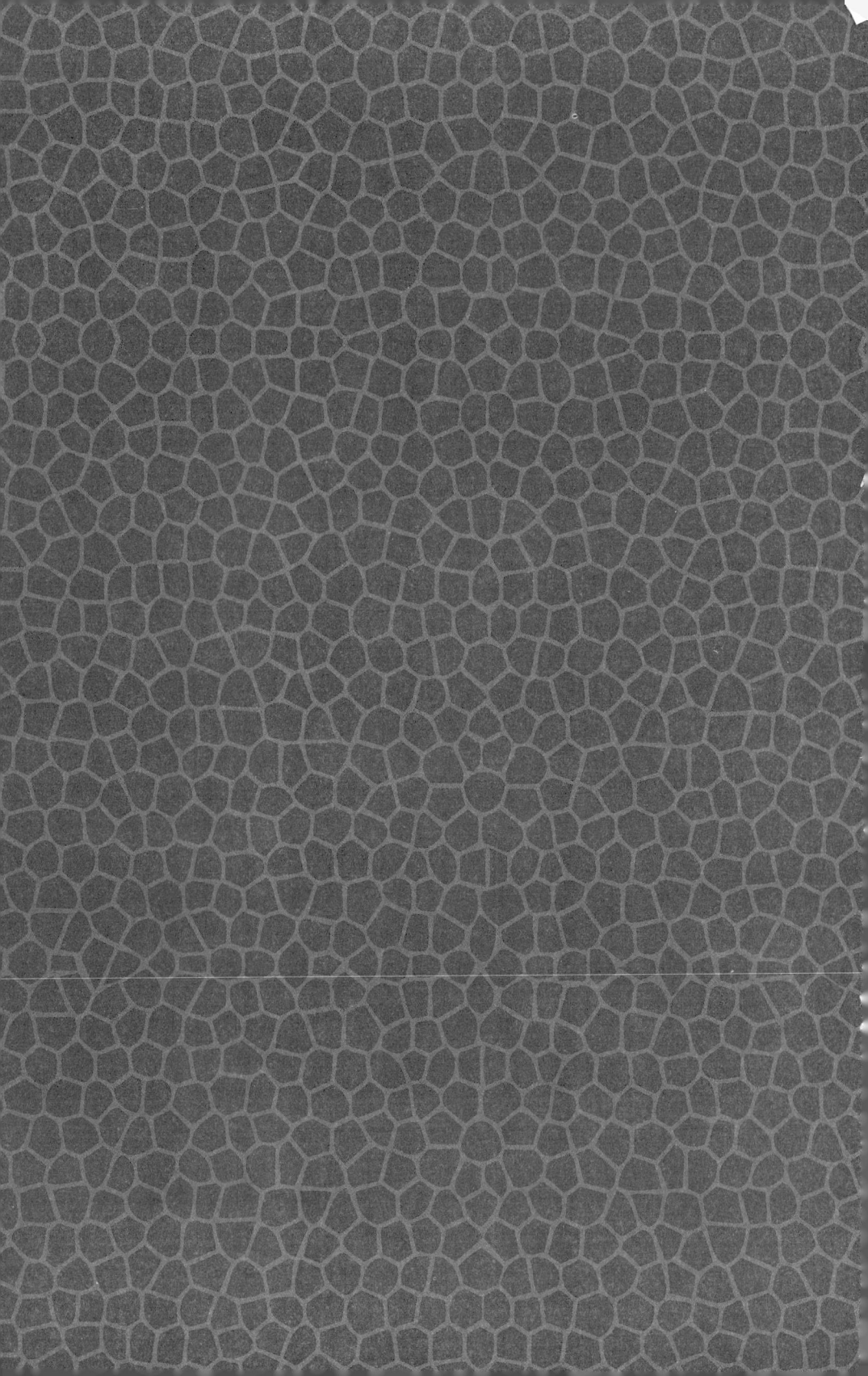